Sisters of Scripture
Mentors in Womanhood

BILLIE MONTGOMERY/COOK

FOREWORD BY JAMES C. PERKINS

JUDSON PRESS
PUBLISHERS SINCE 1824

Join our mailing list for updates and special offers.
www.judsonpress.com/mailing_list.cfm

SISTERS OF SCRIPTURE: Mentors in Womanhood

© 2015 by Judson Press, Valley Forge, PA 19482-0851
All rights reserved.

Judson Press has made every effort to trace the ownership of all quotes. In the event of a question arising from the use of a quote, we regret any error made and will be pleased to make the necessary correction in future printings and editions of this book.

Unless otherwise indicated, Scripture quotations are from the New Revised Standard Version (NRSV), copyright © 1989, Division of Christian Education of the National Council of the Churches of Christ in the United States of America. Used by permission. All rights reserved.

Other versions cited:
The Common English Bible (CEB) © 2011 Common English Bible Used by permission. All rights reserved. The Holy Bible, English Standard Version® (ESV®), copyright © 2001 by Crossway, a publishing ministry of Good News Publishers. Used by permission. All rights reserved.

The Holy Bible, King James Version.
The New American Standard Bible, © 1960, 1962, 1963, 1968, 1971, 1972, 1973, 1975, 1977, 1995 by The Lockman Foundation. Used by permission. The HOLY BIBLE, NEW INTERNATIONAL VERSION®. NIV®. Copyright © 1973, 1978, 1984, 2011 by Biblica, Inc.™ Used by permission. All rights reserved worldwide.

Interior and cover design by Wendy Ronga, Hampton Design Group.

Library of Congress Cataloging-in-Publication Data
Cook, Billie Montgomery. Sisters of scripture: mentors in womanhood/Billie Montgomery Cook.   pages cm
ISBN 978-0-8170-1757-6 (pbk.: alk. paper) 1. Women in the Bible. 2. Women—Religious aspects—Christianity. 3. Christian women—Religious life. I. Title.   BS575.C58 2015
220.9'2082—dc23   2014025827

Printed in the U.S.A.
First printing, 2015.

To Jeanina Sinclair Cook
January 30, 1983—March 7, 2011
(Titus 1:2)
Always and forever our "BOO"

And to my Mom and consummate Mentor,
Alberta W. Montgomery;
I praise God for you and thank you for loving me
in every way that a mother can love a child
and teaching me to do the same with my own.

Likewise, tell the older women
to be reverent in behavior,
not to be slanderers or slaves to drink;
they are to teach what is good,
so that they may encourage the young women.
(Titus 2:3-4)

But a woman who fears the LORD is to be praised.
Give her a share in the fruit of her hands,
and let her works praise her in the city gates.
(Proverbs 31:30-31)

FOREWORD

Billie Montgomery/Cook has a passion for helping young girls realize their potential and live successful, productive lives. In her earlier work, *The Real Deal: A Spiritual Guide for Black Teen Girls* (Judson Press, 2004), she outlined principles to guide young, African American girls in developing their inner beauty and a healthy self-esteem. Here, in her latest work, *Sisters of Scripture: Mentors in Womanhood*, the author highlights the character of certain women of the Bible to help young women see how they can be mentored by these Mothers of our Faith who, though dead, yet speak.

With keen spiritual insight, Ms. Montgomery/Cook has identified life skills that young women need and how they can use the examples of different women of Scripture to serve as examples and mentors to develop those life skills and make those qualities a part of their godly character.

For example, in the first chapter Eve, the author points out that the very temptations Eve faced are the same temptations every woman faces. However, Eve acted impulsively rather than seeking advice from a godly trustworthy source. Thus, Montgomery/Cook highlights how Eve may serve as a cautionary tale for today's young women—an example of how an intelligent and independent woman can allow her strengths to become a weakness.

Throughout this wonderful, insightful book, the author uses the women of the Bible as reliable mentors and trustworthy sources in exploring matters of faith, tackling life challenges, and pursuing character development even at this present day. This is so because human nature has not changed and God's loving compassion toward us has not changed.

This book is a superb resource not only for adolescent girls and young adult women, but also for women's groups and older women who are engaged in mentoring relations with teens and young adults. Ms. Montgomery/Cook writes these chapters not only with spiritual insight and the distilled wisdom of her own life experience, but with the passion to serve as mother-figure, big sister, friend, and spiritual guide to a generation of young ladies who are seeking their way in an increasingly complex world.

She along with these great women of the Bible whose characters she has put on full display—the good, the bad, the ugly, and most of all, the victorious—have achieved that monumental and needed task.

Long live our mothers of the faith! Long live our sisters and our daughters. Thank you, Ms. Montgomery/Cook, for this invaluable resource and compassionate guide.

—Rev. Dr. James C. Perkins
Author, *Playbook for Christian Manhood*
and *Building Up Zion's Walls*
Senior Pastor, Greater Christ Baptist Church
Detroit, Michigan
First Vice President, Progressive National
Baptist Convention, Inc.

PREFACE

One is not born a woman, one becomes one.
—Simone de Beauvoir, The Second Sex, 1949

Is not wisdom found among the aged?
Does not long life bring understanding? (Job 12:12, NIV)

On Monday, March 7, 2011, after an extremely brief illness and the result of an untimely stroke, our beloved daughter, Jeanina Sinclair Cook, died. As we walked out of her hospital room for the last time, dear friends/colleagues from work, G. W. Thompson and Chris Ricks, were waiting. The verbal acknowledgment of what had just happened tumbled from my lips as Chris wrapped me in her arms. "She's gone, Chris, my baby's gone!" I sobbed as she rocked me and held me close.

Within seconds (thanks to our son Joseph), social media spread the news of her passing like fog at the break of day. When we returned home from the hospital after she passed, I collapsed into the arms of my sister-friend Vernelle, who had volunteered to stay at our home to keep watch and serve as telephone secretary. She didn't (couldn't?) speak but cried and held on to me. The phone calls, emails, texts (to Joseph), prayers, and visits to help, console, mourn, and grieve with us came from our Third Baptist Church (Portsmouth, VA) family, from across the country, and from the other side of the planet (my nephew in Japan) like a torrent of rain. In our shock and grief we were moved, humbled, and gratified at the outpouring of love and memory.

On Tuesday, March 8, at 8 a.m., our phone rang. It was Mrs. Virginia Collins, one of the elderly saints of our church, a woman fully acquainted with the pain and agony of planning funerals and burying children and grandchildren.

"Billie?" she said more than asked. "Honey, let's pray," and pray she did. And every morning that week at 8 a.m., Miss Virginia called, I answered, and she prayed. Initially, I couldn't speak, just cried. No, like Jesus, I wept. By Saturday, the day of Jeanina's home-going service, I listened, but a sense of calm and strength replaced the tears. The prayers kept me going each day, all day that week—our first (ever) meeting at a funeral home with staff; choosing her choir robe rather than regular clothes for presentation; selecting a niche at the cemetery for the ashes after cremation (her decision from childhood); picking out pictures and music for the home-going service; responding to the contact from LifeNet that the organ donation (her wish upon getting her driver's license as a teen) and subsequent surgeries had been successful thus far (two men had received her kidneys; her corneas would be given later); and so many other tasks related to saying goodbye and releasing a loved one back to God. The days blurred into each other, but the mornings and the prayers were definite and distinctive.

My best friends for more than forty years, Steph, Renae, and Jan, came from north and south within what seemed to be hours, and (dear) Carolyn joined the group. My sister, Nina, had come a week earlier and had helped me wash Jeanina's hair, the last task we would share as sisters in caring for her before her death. Over the years, especially the teen years of struggle and searching for her place in the world, Nina had served as confidante and mentor to Jeanina. Their friendship was special and went way beyond the niece/aunt bond.

My Mother, despite being close by, called daily and cried and encouraged and prayed. The Saturday before Jeanina passed, she had called the family together (cousins, nieces, nephews, etc.) along with dear family friends Wesley, (Asst.) Pastor Joseph Fleming, etc. to gather in Jeanina's hospital room for prayer, to anoint her body with oil, and to say goodbye. I was reminded that she too had buried a child, my brother Sam, so many years ago.

At one point, during the course of the home-going service, the Spirit led me to look over my left shoulder. "They're here," the Spirit said. "Your sistahs, your posse, is here!" In the balcony on both sides and on one very long church pew were so many of the women in my life who were truly my sisters and sistahs by spirit, experiences, friendship, mutual admiration, and love. It was the group/posse/clan that had shared and exchanged so much love and support to and for each other over the years (our graduations together, births of children and now grandchildren, marriages and divorces, deaths of parents, and now, burying children). Yes, my husband, Keith, and my son, Joseph, were with me every moment, every step, but it was the women who imparted that special aura, that indescribable something only women have to give. At that moment, my heart wept for women who, for whatever reasons, don't like or care for or appreciate women.

This book, the pages that you are holding, is a celebration of women—our gender and our (fairest of the fair) sex. We are a marvelous creation. There is nothing in the world like women. Oh, how God worked to get us just right, for we are a reflection of God's compassion, care, commitment, and love. No wonder woman was the last of God's creative agenda during that very long and exhausting week.

As women, we are at our best when times, circumstances, and conditions demand that we reach beyond our own very narrow grasp and become better than we ever thought we could become. No, not perfect, not yet, but always hoping, loving, doing, caring, and yearning to be the best that we can be—as human creatures, as God's daughters and crowning touch of creation on this side of glory.

To all of the women in my life (you know who you are!) who have shown me what God had in mind when God took that rib from Adam and breathed the breath of life into it, my deepest and heartfelt thanks and praise to God for you. Thank you to the mature saints God has placed in my life at Third Baptist Church—Ms. Virginia Collins; Deaconess Mary Battle; Ms. Mamie Moore; Ms. Doretha Johnson; Ms. Maezelle Johnson; Ms. Rosa Long; Ms. (Frances) Cook; Deacons Mary Hall and Marian Ransom; First Lady Johnnie M. Fleming; the Deaconess Ministry; the Jolly Women's Guild Ministry, and countless more. And for those saints that God has placed in your life to pray for us, lift us up, and teach us the power of prayer as they try their best to serve as mentors to the next generation of prayer partners and prayer warriors (that would be us!), thank you seems so meager and small, but it is all that we have. Thank you, thank you, thank you for your kisses, hugs, words of comfort and support, examples and testimonies of courage, strength, endurance, prayer power, and God's great and precious grace! My sisters, let us marinate, soak in, and soak up their wisdom and their prayers as long as God blesses us with their presence.

To the women/sisters and sistahs at Judson Press (that includes Rebecca, Gale, Tammy, and the rest of the worker bees and prayer partners at Judson) who have come alongside me and kept the dream alive for almost ten years now (yes, it's been that long!), I thank and praise God for you. You are a blessing to me as well.

To my younger sisters who are just beginning the sometimes difficult but never solo journey of learning the beauty and wonder of what it means to be a woman, join us as we continue to hold fast to each other as we hold fast to God, who keeps working on us and will not let us go.

And to ALL of the members of my family (both sides) but especially to William, my Daddy, and to the two male loves of my life, Keith and Joseph, thank you for being you, for giving me time and space to grow, and for loving me unconditionally.

God bless us, every one. —B

INTRODUCTION

My dear one,

We begin by asking and answering a few questions.

We are presently living in the twenty-first century. In the past fifty years, we, as women living in what is called Western culture, have experienced unimagined heights of achievement and acclaim. We have conquered barriers of sexism, racism, and elitism. We have fought and persevered through all kinds of movements and forces: the women's movement, the right to vote, free love, sexual freedom, civil rights, the introduction of the Equal Rights Amendment (which came and went, but keep watching, it'll be back!), and all kinds of generations ("The Greatest," Boomers, X, Y, Me, Millennials, etc.), to name a few. Yes, much time and energy have been given to praying, singing, marching, pleading, begging, demanding, and asserting our right to be heard, felt, obeyed, acknowledged, and regarded, but much continues to be done. Yet, as much as we have accomplished in our free and open society, why resort to studying a time and culture, when the very idea of a woman as a person was the extreme opposite of now?

In other words, why use the Bible as a source for teaching, coaching, assisting, and mentoring young women of today? As much as we, as humans, try to create new ways of living our lives, and as we grow and mature, the more we realize that the new ways we seek aren't new at all. Doesn't the Bible say it best? "There is nothing new under the sun" (Ecclesiastes 1:9). Our motivations are as old as time.

As Christians we believe the Bible still stands as the source of all truth for all humanity. The Bible, God's Word, is timeless and timely; its wisdom is unmatched in human dimension. No other book exists as a source of understanding humankind's choices, decisions, mistakes, and corrections, no matter the century or culture. It is our textbook into learning the personality of God. As beings made in God's image, we must begin as early as possible to read, grow, and develop an interest in studying the Bible, to cultivate a curiosity about the Bible and its relationship to living, as well as to create a desire to be led and guided by its wisdom and direction. In short, as Christians, we must become people of the Word—God's Word.

So who are these women of the Bible? Well, despite the difference of time and place, as we read their stories and think about their lives, we begin to realize that they are us. In so many ways, our commonalities outweigh our differences. It is my sincere hope and desire that these pages will serve as an introduction to a deeper understanding of who we are and who they are as women.

What was life like for women during Old and New Testament times? When compared with our lives, life for them in many ways was incomprehensible in its extreme difficulty. The closest comparisons are seen in the lives of so many of our sisters living in third-world countries. During the desperation and devastation of war or natural disasters and calamities, we are afforded a glimpse into their lives via newspapers, magazines, and the 24/7 news media. From the comfort of our living rooms, we are shocked, appalled, and sometimes overwhelmed at their plight as well as their courage and spirit to fight the human and natural forces that seek to limit and control them.

True, like many of these women of the third world, women during biblical times had few rights as a person; they lacked freedom, the opportunity for education, the voice to determine their own lives; they were considered a male's personal property and were dependent (financially, socially, for security) upon men. For most women, the most valuable part of their bodies was the womb, for it produced children, preferably sons. Biology and culture controlled their lives and determined their destinies and places in the world.

Today, despite all of our technology and movements, have we truly progressed? And what does progress mean? As we look at our current state of biology, culture, and the impact of technology in all of its dimensions, don't we continue to experience many of the same limitations as these early women? Aren't we continuously battling for equality in terms of salaries, career opportunities, advancement, and family structure (care giving, domestic responsibilities)? And what about dating, finding a man, getting a man, keeping a man, and getting the dress? How many television shows, websites, and cellphone apps are focused on those things?

Perhaps we are not as liberated as we believe.

Why study and be mentored by women of the Bible? First, Webster defines a mentor as a trusted counselor or guide. From the time that first young girl experienced her first period, signaling her growth toward womanhood, there were women talking, explaining, guiding, encouraging, nurturing, and mentoring her. It is what we have always done and shall (must?) continue to do as women. It's in our DNA.

Women in the Bible teach us that their basic hopes and dreams are exactly the same as ours. We share the same desires for happiness, love, and peace; if desired, to marry, and to marry someone who truly loves us and will prove faithful to us and protective of us; for those who desire, to have children and to have healthy and happy children; to raise and/or be a significant part of a family; to live in security and protection; to be strong, bold, and courageous when circumstances demand it; and to have full and meaningful lives.

Second, we study women of the Bible because they teach us about relationships—the struggles, good times, and sometimes really bad times between people (males, females, siblings, families, friends, enemies) never change. We learn to understand and face reality, and in facing that reality sometimes we must stand for truth and in courage no matter the outcome.

Third, we study women of the Bible because they teach us the ways that God moves in their and our lives. They show us how God is always present in our lives in spite of our own thoughts, wishes, wants, and desires. They teach us that in spite of and despite all forces designed to keep them oppressed and silent, when we read of women whom God empowered with gifts of intelligence, street smarts, cleverness, strength, and wit, we must stop and pay attention. They demonstrate that God is love, mercy, protection, and provision, and those attributes are timeless and limitless. They also show us despite time and space the consistency of Jeremiah 29:11, as God promises unequivocally, "For surely I know the plans I have for you, says the Lord, plans for your welfare and not for harm, to give you a future with hope." That is a theme that plays out over and over, generation to generation, century to century. It is a theme that shows the timelessness of God and the reason we love and cling to God. As God was their hope, God is our hope.

Fourth, the fact that the Bible is so void of physical descriptions of women in particular clearly demonstrates that it is the inner stuff and not the outside wrapping that counts with God! In comparison, our present-day society can be so enraptured by a woman's physical appearance that quite often we are led to believe that nothing else matters or needs to exist under all of that beauty. Yet, here in the Word, God so clearly sends the message of Proverbs 31:30 (NIV): "Charm is deceptive, and beauty is fleeting; but a woman who fears the Lord is to be praised."

Fifth, let's face it, my darlin', when we read stories of women in the Bible, we're reading scripts of the ultimate reality show. Today's cable stations, videos, online shows, movies—as they say in Brooklyn, fuhgeddaboudit, for they pale in comparison with the drama that unfolds within the pages of the Word!

Sixth, the Word clearly commands us as adults and women to teach our children (Deuteronomy 11:19) and to serve as role models and mentors for younger women (Titus 2:3-4) so that the Word of God continues to be planted, nurtured, and grown to maturity in the generations to come.

Last, the reasons for studying women of the Bible are as many as there are women in the Bible. So let us begin, and despite the fact that volumes and volumes have been written about many of the true giants of womanhood (Eve, Sarah, Mary, the mother of Jesus), we shall try to bring a fresh approach to our discussion of these sistahs. Even with all of the literature, they still have much to teach us.

And yes, you will need a Bible. The version or translation will be your decision (King James Version, New International Version, Contemporary English Version, New Revised Standard Version, The Message). The New Revised Standard Version will be used more than any other translation in this book; however, whatever your choice, keep it handy. A highlighter and small notebook for taking notes would be a good idea as well.

Additionally, as was done in my first book, *The Real Deal: A Spiritual Guide for Black Teen Girls*, Scripture references related to the profiles of these women will be presented at the beginning of each chapter; questions for thought and discussion and sections for prayer (for you and from you) will conclude each chapter.

Finally, we begin our study of the women of the Bible with a word of prayer.

Father God,
You have provided your Word as a source of wisdom, guidance, strength, courage, and direction to us and for us. When we choose to read it and open ourselves to it, Father, you never fail to teach us about you and the ways that you love us and provide for us. Within its pages are guidelines for living a wiser and more abundant life.

As your daughter opens your Word, open her mind, her heart, her spirit, and her understanding to you, your ways, your laws, your personality, and your love. Help her to accept your direction as she learns about women who have lived before her and who have walked where she must walk; women who have been there and done that and leave a cleared path for her to get to you. Help her to see, learn, and understand as they did. Give her a willing spirit to be led by you and to be mentored by them and a longing to make the study of your Word a foundation for living her life. In Jesus' name we pray. Amen.

1

EVE

A Mentor in Personal Responsibility

Genesis 1–3

Welcome to yet another study about the mother of all living! Yet, despite all that has been written about her, we still don't know what Eve looked like. Why? And what does she teach us about responsibility?

Story Synopsis

Genesis, the first book of the Bible, is just that, a book of firsts. Being God as only God is, the Lord takes seven days (some week!) to form and shape the universe—creating light and darkness, the heavens, the oceans, animal life, vegetation. Before the week is over, God creates the man, a human being created to be in God's own image, and names this new creature Adam (which sounds like the Hebrew word for earth, from which the first human was formed, and which, in addition to becoming a proper name, means "human" in the generic sense). Seeing nothing made that could serve as an adequate companion for Adam, God causes him to go into a deep sleep and creates a woman from one of his ribs. The woman, whom Adam eventually names Eve, is created to serve as a "suitable helper" and companion to Adam. Both Adam and Eve share the image of God and are created as equals. Thus, through these two human beings, God creates the concept of marriage, family, companionship, and community. Adam and Eve take residence in the garden of Eden, which God has created for them. By day seven (and week's end), God is resting (whew!).

Despite clear and specific instructions to Adam as to their movement in the garden, in time Eve succumbs to curiosity, impulsiveness, and the suggestive power of a shrewd-talking serpent that convinces her perhaps God wasn't honest about the consequences in regards to a certain tree that stands front and center in the garden of Eden. Perhaps thinking that the serpent could be right, Eve takes a piece of fruit from the very tree that she and Adam have been forbidden to touch. As Adam approaches her, Eve shares the fruit that she has picked and includes Adam in the first act of humanity's disobedience and disregard for God's rules and regulations. As consequences for their disobedience, their fate becomes expulsion from the garden, physical toil for Adam, and pain for Eve in giving birth to children. And then things really go downhill!

Lessons for Life

The Book of Firsts

As stated above, this book of firsts includes quite a list of firsts: the good, the bad, and the ugly. The most important of firsts is that Genesis introduces us to the character and personality of God. We see creative power, artistry, beauty, care, and great attention to detail; the breadth and scope of our world as created through the labor of our God. We see balance (work/rest), provision, order and orderliness, structure and protection. We see the human dimension of God—both masculine and feminine attributes—nurturance and nurturing, patience, love, concern, as well as hurt, disappointment, and the need for discipline. In short, we first see the awesomeness of God!

Second, we see a glimpse of God's first expectation of humankind: that we will be obedient and submissive to God out of love and respect for God and all that God does for us. Think about that: nobody takes care of us like God—nobody!

It Is Character and Not Cup Size That Truly Matters

You can read these passages a hundred times and you will never see a physical description of Eve, or Adam for that matter. Therefore, so many of the images of Eve's physical appearance (long, flowing blonde hair, hourglass figure, 36-DD bra cup size, crystal blue eyes) that we are bombarded with are just that—images from someone's imagination. She could have been black as midnight, golden as polished bronze, or pale as Snow White, tall and athletic or short and voluptuous, statuesque or petite, with tight curls or straight tresses in ebony, mahogany, blonde, auburn, or carrot orange. We don't know, and even if we did, it wouldn't make any difference because God is trying to teach us that it's not her physical appearance but Eve's character that is the most important lesson here. Scripture is clear in speaking about God's disdain for the human preoccupation with the physical/exterior (1 Samuel 16:7) that ignores the true essence of a person—the heart/interior.

No, there are no physical descriptions of Eve recorded in the Bible. To get a close-up of what she looked like is simple. Look into any mirror, and her image will be reflected at you, for you—all women—look just like Eve.

So get used to it and stop trying to do things to yourself (whatever the fashion police, Madison Avenue designers, pop teen idols, or social media dictate is the thing of the week to do), thinking that you're somehow improving on what God has created. No, you were created with all of the attributes that God intended for you and Eve to have and to share. Deal with it, accept it, and be proud of what God has done for you. Remember: Our Creator makes no mistakes!

But Wait! There's More!

When in doubt, if (and when) faced with a crucial decision, seek a second opinion from a knowledgeable and trustworthy source. Isn't it interesting that we never see Eve ask Adam or God for an opinion about what the serpent told her? First, when she took its words at face value and proceeded to eat of the fruit, her actions demonstrated disobedience, a great lack of wisdom, a tendency to act impulsively, and a desire for more. Influenced by the serpent, Eve concluded that the "tree was good for food, and . . . was a delight to the eyes, and . . . was to be desired to make one wise" (Genesis 3:6). The serpent served up the wisdom part of it almost as if that were a bonus. That part of it—the wisdom to become just like God—became the real temptation.

Second, Eve's story shows how sometimes our ignorance, naiveté, greed, lack of wisdom, and haste can send a message to others (serpents?) of our vulnerability. In other words, we can be used, abused, and exploited. When you have to make decisions, especially major decisions, don't move too quickly.

Never allow people to talk or push you into anything—no matter how friendly they appear to be. Seek God's wisdom and opinion, and let the Spirit lead you to the knowledgeable and trustworthy source that our Creator has placed in your life to help you. Because, darlin', the serpents are out there watchin' and waitin'!

It's Partnership, Not Boss-ship

The passages that relate to the creation of woman (Genesis 1:26-28; 2:21-24) recount the time, care, and attention that God spends on her. First, like Adam, she is created in the image of God (Genesis 1:26-27). This is important stuff because it shows man and woman were created to stand as equals before God.

Second, Eve is created from one of Adam's ribs (Genesis 2:21-23), the place closest to Adam's heart and from his side. This offers a powerful metaphor for how women and men are intended to stand in relation to one another and before God: side by side, not with one behind or underfoot. Finally, Eve is created to be Adam's helper and companion (Genesis 2:18)—and the Hebrew word for "helper" is the same word used often in Scripture to name God as Israel's helper. Thus, the creation of woman as a suitable helper ("help meet," KJV) is not in the least a secondary or subservient role. Indeed, nothing else in the universe compares with her, and nothing else is created after her. She is the crowning touch of creation.

Third, when the serpent appears to Eve and suggests that she act in disobedience to God's rule and order, we are witnessing the first strike against humanity's submission to God. As long as Adam and Eve proved obedient to God's orders, their protection, care, and provision—their innocence—

were assured. Once their obedient will was destroyed (the introduction of sin), their bond with God was broken.

So it is with us and our marriages. When we break the bond of submission to God as we pursue our own selfish agendas (total focus on the wedding and not the marriage; repeating vows before God that we know we won't keep; doing our own thing; creating our own rules), the bonds of marriage between husband and wife are broken as well, and marriage as God intends no longer exists.

Our husbands must view us as their wives and as their helpers, intended to be partners in the labors of life. Women were created as a gift from God, an equal partner who brings different views, opinions, skill sets, and strengths to the union to build and strengthen the union. In short, this partnership is called mutual submission—for both wife and husband (Ephesians 5:15-33). As we learn to submit ourselves to each other, we then learn how to submit ourselves to God. In short, marriage becomes a partnership between equals who recognize and understand that their individual strengths bring unity to their mutual submission to God's will for their marriage and their lives.

Think about it, and don't get it twisted: as daughters of God, women deserve husbands who are godly and understand who God is and are willing to be followers and imitators of Christ's example in loving their wives so that the Lord can lead, guide, and bless our marriages and families with the best that only God can give. It is why God does the mating selections. It is the Creator's way of replicating, once again, the garden of Eden (protection, provision, security) in a marriage. It is the great lesson that Adam and Eve teach us: the penalty for messin' up that relationship with God!

Additionally, the story of Adam and Eve even goes beyond the boundaries of marriage. Remember that with Adam and Eve came the concept of family and community. They represent a valuable lesson for all human beings, no matter what their status might be—single, married, single again, or remarried. When the Creator observed that it was not good for the man/human being to be alone, God was making an observation that is true for all people, at all stages in life and relationship. We were not created in isolation. We were created for community—to be in relationship with others who will walk with us in this journey of life and faith. Therefore, whether you have found that special someone with whom you can share a future in covenant marriage, whether you are still awaiting that future spouse, or whether you are following the Lord one on one, Genesis 1:2 declares that you are not alone. God intends for you to have companions and companionship along the way—helpers suitable for your journey, other women and men who may be family members, friends, co-workers, and brothers and sisters in Christ. Welcome and embrace your companions with the same joy and jubilation that Adam expressed when he recognized in Eve someone who was made of the same stuff and intended for the same purpose: to love God and bring glory to the Lord all the days of their and our lives.

Did She Really Desire to Be First at This?

Finally, we can't leave the discussion of Eve without acknowledging her first status, not only as the first woman to experience the pains of labor and delivery in childbirth (yeah, she probably cursed that serpent then, huh, as most women in the midst of childbirth do!) but also to experience the anguish of the death of a child (Genesis 4:1-8,25). Eve is forced to endure the ultimate nightmare of any and all parents: the violent death of one child at the hands of a sibling, and the loss of that other child, who was consumed and overtaken by sin.

The story of the embattled brothers, Cain and Abel, plays out in today's headlines much too often. We see the tears, despair, and inconsolable grief on the countenances of too many of our sisters when they are faced with these kinds of horrific tragedies. What words exist to describe the interior of a mother's heart when these things happen? How does one begin to explain the nature of such horror? We can only imagine the kinds of internal chaos and trauma these kinds of incidents create in families, yet these situations and the parents who must endure these tragedies exist among us. Many are in our own families. Yes, these are our siblings, cousins, classmates, and friends who are dying in record numbers, but it is also our parents, grandparents, siblings, co-workers, and friends who are identifying bodies and making those funeral arrangements.

According to the latest report from the Centers for Disease Control, homicide was the number one cause of death for black males ages fifteen to thirty-four.[1] Young black males die from gun violence at a rate 2.5 times higher than Latino males and 8 times higher than white teens.[2] That's a lot of brothers killing brothers and an ocean of tears shed by an awful lot of Eves.

Yes, we live in a violent culture in these United States and in this world. The flip side of this catastrophe is the loss of Cain and others like him to a mindset that chooses murder as the ultimate statement of revenge, no matter the slight, grievance, or offense. Therefore, along with the rising numbers of homicide victims are equally rising numbers of black men caught in the vise of the country's criminal justice system.

More than 60 percent of the people in prison are now racial and ethnic minorities.[3] Among black males in their thirties, one in every ten is in prison or jail on any given day. The number of women in prison, a third of whom are incarcerated for nonviolent drug offenses, is increasing at nearly double the rate for men. Additionally, a smaller percentage of black women are being incarcerated, and that decrease is almost matched by the increase of white women who are going to prison.[4] What is going on here?

In short, in terms of the loss of children's lives and their futures, the mothers and grandmothers, Eves of the world, are crying tears exponentially. Dare we even mention the children caught in this madness who have lost fathers, mothers, and other loved ones to death and incarceration? What about their futures and the effect on our communities, society, and nation?

Yes, Eve goes on to have another child, Seth. But could the pain of the first children ever go away? As a biblical mentor, Eve teaches us many things about being a woman, a wife, and a mother. As we live and grow, each and every day, we learn new things about her, and as a result we learn new things about ourselves.

Last, the study of Eve forces us to stop from time to time and examine our own character. Under all of that hair, makeup, and designer whatever, who are you as a person, as a woman? Who are you as a wife or mother, as a worker or friend? When God raises you up in the mornings and you look in the mirror, what is reflected? What characteristics do you live by and present to the world? As a daughter of God, is your Creator pleased with your representation of the divine image in you? Yes, the Lord forgives, but just as God did with Eve and Adam, God holds us responsible for our actions, behaviors, and choices.

Questions

1. In physical terms, give your own imaginative description of both Adam and Eve. What influences your thoughts about their appearance?

2. Describe the character traits of both Adam and Eve. As humans, do we continue to demonstrate those character traits or have we evolved beyond that?

3. Do you agree or disagree with God's punishment for Adam and Eve's disobedience? Why or why not? What do you think should have been their punishment?

4. How do you think God should punish you for your disobedience? Read Psalm 103.

5. Read Ephesians 5:21-33. How is the marriage relationship described? How have you seen this image distorted in your experience or the relationships around you?

6. In Genesis 4:9, Cain asks, "Am I my brother's keeper?" Are we our brother's (and sister's) keeper? Why or why not?

7. Read the opening Scripture passages again. In which verse do Adam and Eve apologize to God for their actions? In this case, do you think apologies make a difference?

A Prayer for You

Creator God, how mind-blowing, wonderful, and awe-inspiring it is to read of your greatness, to learn of your design and desire for our universe, our world, and us as human beings, created in your image. To think about it leaves us breathless, humbled, wondering, and questioning. Why do you choose to love us, provide for us, protect us, and bless us when over and over again we have fallen so far short of what you deserve from us? As Adam and Eve did so clearly, we continue to repeat their same mistakes, but as you loved them even in their disobedience to you, so you continue to love us.

So, God, we ask that of you now. Don't stop loving us and forgiving us, and don't give up on us. Help your daughter to grow day by day to understand and embrace the joys of submission to your way and your will for her. Lift her head, hold her close, and speak to her when she would be influenced or swayed by the serpents of this world who wish nothing good or positive for her. Remind her of Eve's mistake so that she will have the insight to do what Eve neglected to do: call on you for guidance, wisdom, and forgiveness when she does wrong.

Remind her daily that the same way that you provided a garden of Eden for Adam and Eve for their shelter, protection, and provision, you have also set aside the same for her because your grace, mercy, and love are the best of Eden! In Jesus' name we pray. Amen.

A Prayer from You

Notes

1. Centers for Disease Control, "Leading Causes of Death by Age Group of Black Males in the United States, 2009," www.cdc.gov/nchs.
2. Children's Defense Fund, "Protect Children, Not Guns 2012," www.blackyouthproject.com.
3. Bureau of Justice report (2011), cited at the Sentencing Project, www.sentencingproject.org.
4. www.hereandnow.wbur.org/2013/03/28/women-prison-racial.

2

SARAH AND HAGAR

Mentors in Trust

Genesis 16:1–18:15; 21:1-21

Something special happens when women support each other, but take cover when they don't!

Story Synopsis

We're still in the book of Genesis and still in the book of firsts. By Genesis 12, we meet Abram and watch as he receives the call and is challenged by God: "Go from your country and your kindred and your father's house to the land that I will show you. I will make of you a great nation, and I will bless you, and make your name great, so that you will be a blessing" (Genesis 12:1-2). That's quite a promise to someone whom God, in time, will identify as a "friend" (James 2:23).

In obedience, Abram leaves his father's house and takes his wife, Sarai, and all of his possessions, and settles in Canaan. Things, however, get a little complicated when folks begin to tinker around with the "make of you a great nation" part of the promise. Sarai, Abram's wife, although described as beautiful, is also barren and is well beyond her childbearing years. To help God's promise of nationhood become a reality, Sarai decides to have Abram father children through her maid, Hagar. Hagar, in turn, gets pregnant and has a son, Ishmael. The drama begins to unfold between Sarai and Hagar when Hagar gets a big head over the fact that she now has the son and Sarai doesn't. It gets even more dramatic when God eventually keeps that promise to Abram (now Abraham), and Sarai (now called Sarah) does get pregnant and has a son. With the arrival of Isaac, Sarah declares that Hagar and Ishmael have to go, and Abraham agrees to send them away.

In the midst of Hagar's desperation of forced homelessness and exile, God appears to Hagar and promises her that she and her son will be cared for. Through Ishmael, the Arab nation is born and the hostility between Israel/the Jewish nation and the Arab nation begins and continues to this day. And you thought today's baby mama drama can get crazy!

Lessons for Life

Help Wanted?

If and when God needs our help, the Lord will call us. From the minute Sarah hears the discussion of God's promise to Abram of a son for them (Genesis 18:9-15), she is convinced that it's a joke with her and Abram as innocent victims. She looks at their circumstances (their ages, as well as her post-menopausal status) and sees nothing else. In essence, Sarah doesn't trust God's promise. She makes the major mistake of placing human limits on a God who is limitless in power, might, and authority. She forgets that God is in control and runs things.

How often do we do the same thing—limit God to what we can see via our human eyes rather than believing that God can and will do what God says, despite the odds, the negative talk, our dismissive attitudes, and our smaller-than-a-mustard-seed faith? Don't get it twisted or confused, my darlin'. The Lord is God (Isaiah 55:8-9).

A New Name, a New Role, a New Life

Genesis 17:5 describes the conversation God has with Abram in which the Lord informs him of the divine plan for Abram and the family that he will have. God changes Abram's name to Abraham, "father of many nations," and vows to bless Abraham through those nations. In a similar manner, in Genesis 17:15, God tells Abraham that Sarai's name will change to Sarah, "mother of nations" (the only woman in the Bible to have her named changed by God). This is another example of God's awesomeness and divine vision for two people, imperfect but obedient to God's will for their lives!

You Thought Surrogates Were a Modern Concept?

Ecclesiastes 1:9 reminds us that there is nothing new under the sun. Although controversial even today, the idea of gestational carriers or surrogate mothers is far from new. Today, women now have the opportunity to volunteer as well as to be paid to perform this act of reproductive support to women who are unable to conceive or carry a child to term in their pregnancies. With the help of medical technology, more and more women are serving as genetically unrelated surrogates by providing a womb to nurture other people's children. But in Abram's and Sarai's time, surrogacy was also a common practice, possibly seen as a way to fulfill the creation mandate to fill the earth and subdue it. And there are other biblical patriarchs and matriarchs who practiced surrogacy as well. Most notably, when they struggled with maternal fertility, Leah and Rachel both gave their maidservants, Bilhah and Zilpah, to Jacob, and together, the four women became mothers of the twelve tribes of Israel.

It does bear notice that these maidservants were "given to" the patriarchs. What they were not given was a choice in the matter. As Sarai's maidservant, all decisions were made for Hagar, and her womb was volunteered (voluntold?) to bear Abram's child for Sarai. Further, because Scripture tells us that Hagar wasn't simply a household servant but an Egyptian slave, she probably had even fewer liberties than other maidservants may have enjoyed. As the expectant mother of the wealthy Abram's long-desired son, perhaps she imagined that her status would change when the child she carried was born. It is understood that quite often women in her position would have found themselves elevated to the position of senior wife, thus displacing their former (now lesser) mistresses in the household's hierarchy after such a birth.

In ancient times, the act of surrogacy was so important yet delicate an issue that the senior wife would stand behind the surrogate during childbirth and brace the laboring woman during contractions, serving as a human birthing chair. In the case of Leah, when she describes Bilhah, her maidservant, giving birth "upon my knees," the baby would have been delivered in Leah's lap (Genesis 30:3). The relationship between the women was just that close.

Sorry, Hagar, but that didn't happen here.

Abram's love for Sarai was so deep that when Hagar got uppity about bearing the son, Abram stepped back and gave Sarai free rein, as in, "She's all yours; deal with her as you wish."

Unintended Consequences

Sarah's creation of Hagar's act of surrogacy and the subsequent birth of Ishmael to Abraham sets off a long, intense series of circumstances that Sarah could never have envisioned when she first thought of having a baby through Hagar. Ironically, even tragically, given God's plans for their future, this act of surrogacy wasn't necessary. And when given the opportunity to make Hagar and Ishmael full members of the family (as Jacob, Leah, and Rachel were able to do with Bilhah and Zilpah), Sarah and Abraham chose to do the opposite: they throw Hagar and her son, Ishmael, out of the house, thus abandoning them to homelessness. Because Hagar tried to elevate herself and because Sarah rejected the son of Hagar instead of adopting Ishmael as her own, Abraham became the father not of two tribes of a united people but of two separate nations forever at war with each other.

Ishmael grew up and entered into manhood, married, had twelve sons of his own, and lived a long life (Genesis 25:14-17). His descendants brought forth the Arab nation. In other words, Hagar was ultimately as blessed with as many sons as Sarah was. You do know that Sarah never saw that comin', don'cha?

Our Desperation Is God's Specialty

Despite the fact that Sarah's and Hagar's relationship fell apart and Hagar was forced to leave the security of the home that she shared with Abraham and Sarah, God appeared to Hagar in the wilderness, offering assurance that she and her son would be cared for. Her cries of anguish and despair (Genesis 16:9-14) were answered with provision and sanctuary.

God's assurance of care to Hagar is Exhibit A of how God takes care of us when we, as in Hagar's situation, have nowhere whatsoever to turn. Think about her plight: she was unmarried, a single mother, homeless, and without a job. How familiar does that sound? Hagar concluded that her only recourse was to die. God showed up to assure her that death was not a part of the divine plan. The Lord knew her status and understood her needs. Hagar listened, heeded, believed, and—unlike Sarah—trusted God's promise. God, in turn, took care of her and Ishmael.

The greater lesson here? No matter how dire and dark our circumstances appear to be in this life, we, just like Hagar, must turn to God for all of our needs, trusting and believing what the Lord says. And although Sarah saw an opportunity to be careless and thoughtless in Hagar's demise, God worked it out for Hagar's good.

Sistah to Sistah?
Our greatest ally and worst enemy? When Sarah created the solution to the problem of getting offspring for Abraham, she turned to the closest person to her, another woman, Hagar, her maidservant. Who else would know her better? Who else but Hagar knew Sarah's heartache of barrenness, was witness to the grief of month after month, year after year, discovering that she was not pregnant? Who else but Hagar could have been included in this family drama?

Yet, when things began to fall apart, it is the relationship between those two women that came into question.

It was not a question of jealousy in terms of love, for Sarah knew that Abraham loved her and only her; however, jealousy, insecurity, and hierarchy based on sons became the weapons of mass destruction in this relationship between women.

All of this begs the question: Suppose Sarah had not intervened and tweaked the plans of God? Suppose things had been allowed to run their natural course and Sarah had stayed in her lane? Can you imagine the wonder, excitement, and joy that Hagar could have shared with Sarah as she bore a son in her old age? It was the confirmation of God's promises as true and unchanging, despite what we think, feel, or see. Oh, how those two women could have rejoiced together.

Something mysterious and wonderful happens when women get together. It is the energy, the power, the beauty, the wonder of it all when women come together, especially for a common cause. How much knowledge, love, wisdom, and care materialize when women fill a room? How many churches, organizations, and schools are designed, funded, built, and maintained when women make the conscious decision to meet and conquer a need or concern? What happens when women come together to pray?

Regrettably, Sarah and Hagar are an example of the worst that can happen when things fall apart between women. Their sons, however, are examples of what God can make happen despite circumstances and relationships of birth, when children can put those things of separation aside and come together for a common good. Isaac, son of Abraham and Sarah, joins with Ishmael, son of Abraham and Hagar, his half-brother, to bury their father (Genesis 25:9). We also learn that after the death of Sarah, Abraham marries again, and he and his new wife, Keturah, have six sons (Genesis 25:1-2). Talk about nation building!

Questions

1. List some things that Scripture promises us as God's children (see 2 Corinthians 6:14–7:1).
2. In view of this story, consider this quote (from the Disney Studio film *The Santa Clause*): "Seeing isn't believing, believing is seeing." Read Hebrews 11:1. Is this the same thing? Why or why not?
3. List some things that you believe that God has promised you.
4. What happens when women come together and pray?

A Prayer for You

Lord God, we give you thanks for the women you have raised up to be in our lives—our mothers, grandmothers, aunts, cousins, sisters, and girlfriends. We are so grateful that when you made us as women, you placed in our spirits the spirit of kinship, caring, concern, strength, great love, and friendship. When women gather, you are truly in our midst!

God, we pray for your daughter and the kind of woman she is destined to be. Let her see you move in her life as she makes friends and takes her place among and in the midst of other women. Let her show friendship, love, and caring as she grows and develops. Help her to understand how special it is to be a woman in the midst of other women. Keep her from the negativity that can come between women to rob us of our peace and destroy the bond between us. Help her to understand that such negativity is not of you but of the evil one who would destroy and tear down. Teach her that he has no power and your plans for her are far greater than Satan could ever imagine. In Jesus' name we pray. Amen.

A Prayer from You

3

THE DAUGHTERS OF LOT

Mentors in Hope

Genesis 19–20

The story of Lot and his two nameless daughters reads like a sordid soap opera. And that's just the part before they leave Sodom!

Story Synopsis

After many warnings, God makes the final pronouncement on the city of Sodom: it will be destroyed due to the extreme wickedness of its inhabitants. Lot, the nephew of Abraham, has built a life for himself and his family in the midst of Sodom and all of its depravity. When it comes time for the city to be destroyed, God agrees to send two angels to warn Lot and remove his family to safety. When residents of the city discover that Lot has given housing and refuge to two strangers, they surround his home and demand that Lot turn the guests over to them. Lot offers his two daughters to the men of Sodom instead. The men refuse, and then things really get crazy! The angels pull Lot back into the house; the men of Sodom are blinded by the angels so that they can't find the door to the house; and by dawn, Lot and his family are out of Sodom. By nightfall, the cities of Sodom and Gomorrah are in ashes, Mrs. Lot is a pillar of salt, and Lot and his two daughters have to begin their new lives in a cave.

As strange as all of that sounds, pay attention, my darlin', because this is where things begin to get weird.

As Lot and his daughters set up housekeeping in the cave, the older daughter begins to think about all of the things that she and her sister are missing in Sodom: companionship, men, the opportunity to marry and raise families. Her focus on what they are missing, rather than what they have (security, protection from Sodom, provision from God), leads her to think of desperate acts. She decides that because she and her sister are stuck in a cave with their father and because they will never have the opportunity to meet men, marry, and have children, they should have sex with their dad. She shares this idea with her younger sister, who agrees. According to the Word, they manage to get their father, Lot, drunk and take turns having sex with him. The result is that both sisters get pregnant and have children by him.

Now, stand back and think about that. This is a pretty desperate thing to do, and it creates all kinds of questions. Aside from, What was she thinking? the second most important question becomes, How could these young women have known that they would never meet men? 'Cause never is a very long time!

This story is important because, despite its age, it's timeless. Way back in the day (around 1985—yeah, that far back), a few educators at Harvard and Yale Universities came up with a statistic related to women with college degrees (www.snopes.com). They surmised that a woman over the age of forty with a college degree had a better chance of being killed by a terrorist than of finding a husband and getting married! Yes, you read that right. You can't begin to imagine the panic and desperation that statistic started. It was false and flawed, but many women believed it and felt they were doomed to a life of loneliness and frustration. News stories and magazine articles began to feed into the frenzy with stories about where women could find a man (Alaska, Wyoming, North Dakota, etc.). And if you were a black, college-educated woman, the statistics were even worse. We couldn't even get a terrorist to think about looking for us so they could shoot us. At some historically black colleges and universities, the ratio between women and men can be around 10:1, which is great for the guys but perceived as catastrophic for the women. With stats like that, what's a woman to do?

Lessons for Life

Stay Away from "Desperately Thinking" about Anything

There has always been some notion pushing women into panic mode as it relates to men. Many women continue to think that if they aren't married by a certain age they are doomed to a life of unhappiness. Therefore, to counter that fear, they feel that they must take matters into their own hands to find a mate. Don't let the enemy create such an environment of desperation, frustration, anger, and vulnerability in your life. God controls your future. Jeremiah 29:11 reassures us that God and only God knows the Lord's plans for each and every one of us. If it is God's will that you marry,

God has already made all necessary arrangements (the mate, how you will meet). Trust the Lord and not some pseudoscientific statistic.

Marriage and family were created by God. Such covenant love is part of our Creator's design for civilization to continue. As long as God is, love, companionship, marriage, and family will continue to exist. Trust and believe that.

Review Your History with God from Time to Time

There isn't a single point in the story of Lot's daughters where Scripture states that these young women ever thought about asking God to provide for their futures. Isn't it possible that the same God who was concerned enough and powerful enough to rescue them from the destruction of a city would also be concerned enough and powerful enough to give them a future—complete with a loving spouse and family?

At times in our lives, we have to sit down and think about all the places that God has brought us and decide that because God has provided in our past, God will provide in our future.

Don't Bring the Worst of the Past into God's Future for You

In this story, when Lot and his family were rescued from the burning city of Sodom, the angels told them not to look back. All listened but one, Lot's wife, and she was turned into a pillar of salt due to her disobedience.

When Lot's daughters came up with the idea of having children by their father, they too were looking back and bringing the worst with them. They were returning to the kind of desperation and wickedness they grew up seeing in Sodom. How can God move us forward if we fail to release the harm of the past? The daughters of Lot are our mentors by teaching us what *not* to do—and thus reminding us that our future lies in the confident assurance of God's love and provision for us. That is our hope (Psalm 33:18-22).

Questions

1. Who was Lot? What was his family structure?
2. Why did God delay in destroying Sodom?
3. Why does God delay in punishing us? Why does God delay in punishing you?
4. What does this story teach us about environment and its influences?
5. List some behaviors that women engage in today that are perceived as desperately seeking a man.
6. Read Job 8:13. How does this apply to the story of Lot's daughters?

A Prayer for You

Creator God, we lift your daughter up to you this day. We pray for her growth in you and toward you. Teach her to not get sidetracked by the doom-and-gloom naysayers of life in regard to her future. Open her eyes to the bright and positive future that you have set aside for her. Reassure her in moments of doubt and fear that you surround her and hold her up. Keep her calm and focused on the work that she is doing, be it coursework in school, housework at home, or paid work in the profession that you have given her, daily reminding her that she works first for you and then people. In Jesus' name we pray. Amen.

A Prayer from You

4

LEAH AND RACHEL

Mentors in Self-Worth

Genesis 29–30

Lyrics to an Irving Berlin song called "Sisters" caution any "mister" who puts himself between two sisters—and warns the sister who tries to interfere with the relationship her sibling has with a man![1] Those lyrics pretty much introduce us to the biblical sisters Leah and Rachel.

Story Synopsis

The story of Leah and Rachel is one of family and sisterhood with a few subplots within it. The first is an ode to all of the older sisters of the world who find that they must play second best to their more beautiful, more popular, or more talented younger sisters. The second deals with the intricacies of love and what it means to love and to be "in love." The third is a word to women who choose to create attachments to men via children, thinking that it is the way to love.

Submitting to his mother's wish that he should marry within the family, Jacob (the grandson of Abraham and Sarah and the younger son of Isaac and Rebekah) travels to Paddan-aram, his mother's childhood home. There he meets and falls head over heels in love with Rachel, a daughter of his uncle Laban (Rebekah's brother). Perhaps seeing an opportunity to take advantage of a lovesick young man, Laban initially agrees to Jacob's request to marry Rachel in exchange for seven years of unpaid labor. The morning after his long-awaited wedding night, however, Jacob discovers that Laban has tricked him and replaced his intended bride, Rachel, with her older sister, Leah. The Bible doesn't explain why Jacob doesn't notice the switch until morning, so I'm guessing that it must have really been dark in that tent. Where's modern lighting when you need it?

Claiming the importance of tradition, Laban convinces Jacob that he still can marry Rachel, if Jacob agrees to work for him an additional seven years. Jacob agrees and then marries Rachel. He is now a man with two wives who are sisters, who also bring into the marriage their two hand-maids, Bilhah and Zilpah. (Remember we mentioned them in chapter 2?)

From day one, Leah knows that Jacob is in love with her sister, Rachel. Jacob doesn't hide it; he doesn't diminish it; he doesn't deny it or apologize for it. He adores Rachel and always has. Leah also knows that Jacob was tricked into marrying her. She soon learns something else: that she can have children and her sister, Rachel, can't. For Leah, the factor of children makes her realize that her value to Jacob has risen exponentially. "If I can give him sons," she figures, "then he will love me." The race to bear children is on!

From day one as well, Rachel is keenly aware of Jacob's love and that he loves her regardless of her limitations. There are no instances in the Bible story which suggest that Rachel taunted Leah for being the unloved wife. Perhaps she didn't have to. We do see, however, that Rachel's insecurities about her barren status create much tension and confusion between these two sisters. Things get so competitive that at one point, Rachel demands that either Jacob give her a child or she'll die.

The Scripture covers a lot of time in not many verses, with a lot of babies being conceived and born. We can imagine each woman's feelings about the sisters' relationship with each other and with Jacob based on how they named each child (Genesis 29:31–30:24). Leah's naming of her first four sons is particularly heart-wrenching (see Genesis 29:31-35). Eventually, when things settle down in the tumultuous household and a final head count is made, Leah has produced six sons, Reuben, Simeon, Levi, Judah, Issachar, and Zebulun, and one daughter, Dinah (Jacob's one and only). Acting as Leah's surrogate, the maidservant Zilpah produces two more sons, Gad and Asher, by Jacob. Rachel's surrogate, Bilhah, also produces two sons by Jacob, Dan and Naphtali. Only after the other women in the household have given birth to ten boys and one girl does Rachel finally conceive and delivers a child of her own, a son she calls Joseph. Later, she dies in childbirth after naming this son Ben-oni, "son of my sorrow." Jacob renames the son Benjamin. These twelve sons of Jacob evolve to become the twelve tribes of Israel.

Enduring morning sickness, weight gains and losses, painful contractions and dangerous deliveries, Leah presented Jacob with seven children. When her last son was born, Leah said, "Now my husband will honor me, because I have borne him six sons" (Genesis 30:20). She had certainly earned that much from her husband over the years, and it seems reasonable to assume that Jacob did love Leah, but neither time nor the presentation of a half-dozen male heirs did anything to change the fact that Jacob was in love with Rachel. Everyone recognized that fact, even the children, because Jacob carried that preferential affection into his relationship with his sons, favoring Rachel's sons, Joseph and Benjamin, over the others.

Yes, my dear one, there is a significant difference between loving and being in love. There's an old song that Tony Bennett popularized when he croons that he can't explain why he loved the object of his affection. He just loved her! That, my darlin', sums up the nature of Jacob's relationship with Rachel. He just loves her. Well, why is it that we love the people that we love, particularly those with whom we are in relationship? Sometimes we can point to specific things—their smile, their character, their kindness, their thoughtfulness, their quirks or habits. And sometimes we don't know what it is. It just is!

Lessons for Life

Is It the Female DNA?

What is it about sisters that make our sibling relationships such a roller-coaster ride of emotions and vulnerabilities? Yes, our brothers have their own list of competitions and rivalries, but sisters tend to bring a unique set of issues. Ask any two (or group) of sisters about how they get along and you'll probably get a range of anywhere from "very close," to "it depends on the day or time," to "distant and don't care." It's the roller coaster!

For some of us, time, family crises, dysfunction, circumstances, and distance have molded and shaped who we are and how we now relate to each other, not only as family members but also as sisters. For others, our parents have mandated a definition of what our relationships should look like within as well as outside the family unit. For still others, our needs and great desire to be in harmony and good relationship with our family member of the same gender and experiences guide and shape our sense of sisterhood.

In the case of Leah and Rachel, the Bible yields little indication of the kind of relationship these two sisters shared in childhood. We can only hope that they were sister-friends and playmates, loving, protecting, and caring for each other. But we still must ask ourselves, At what point did things change for them? We do know that Rachel was the beautiful one and Leah the plain one. Let's face facts: Leah and Rachel didn't wake up one morning as teens to suddenly discover the differences in their appearances. That kind of distribution of physical attributes becomes a point of discussion and comparison within and outside the family at birth! Whether we are pretty or plain, folks have a way of quickly alerting us to our strengths and weaknesses, pluses and minuses much earlier than we are emotionally ready to deal with them. Many of us carry those burdens all of our lives. For those of us unable to overcome, accept, or make peace with the reality of our physical situation or limitations, the result can be jealousy, anger, and bitterness even into adulthood. It can affect and color or distort our relationships with each other. These two sisters force us to look at ourselves and our own sisters and our relationship with each other. Do we get along? Why or why not? What must be said, dealt with, or confronted to make the relationship better? From that beginning, we then must look at our relationships with other sisters, those beyond our families. Are there petty jealousies and envy? If so, why do we allow them to exist and destroy what could be solid and emotionally valuable relationships?

Sometimes You've Just Got to Suck It Up and Deal with It

For Leah and those of us who strongly identify with her, the idea of being unloved, particularly by the one we believe is the one for us, is a bitter pill to swallow. Even as she labors to bring forth new life, Leah recognizes that her motivation to win Jacob's heart is a hopeless struggle and a lost cause. That battle was over the minute Jacob laid eyes on Rachel. Even today, how often does a woman pursue a similar attachment to a man, thinking that a child or children will cement her place in his heart only to have him abandon her and prefer or turn to someone else?

As difficult as life can be, sometimes we must accept what is and go on with our lives—even in matters of the heart. And in living our lives, sometimes we must grow to understand that the one hasn't been presented as yet. Stay faithful and stay focused. When and if it is in God's plan for you to meet the one, God will make it so and you won't have to design any tricks and schemes or let desperation put you in panic mode for it to happen. Most importantly, a child won't have to be an ingredient in the cement to hold the man to you.

Leah's story also forces us to examine our own unique definitions of love and all of the many ways that we can express our love toward the one as well as toward family, friends, sister-friends, colleagues, and others we consider loved ones. It forces us to assess and embrace the kinds of things that we need to live full, rich, loving, and complete lives.

Game Change!

The third lesson this story teaches us is about the children who find themselves caught up in these situations.

Rachel eventually bears a son with Jacob, and she names him Joseph. After Rachel's death, Jacob's love and regard for her becomes focused on her firstborn son. Jacob has ten other sons by Leah and the surrogates, but he acts as though none of them exist but Joseph, favoring him over the older brothers, giving him special gifts, and making no secret of his preference.

Jacob's blatant favoritism of Joseph creates absolute chaos and confusion in this extended family of sisters, brothers, wives, and maidservants. Further, it sets off a chain of events that boggles the mind in its dramatic intrigue, twists, and turns (Genesis 37–50). In fact, it becomes the stuff of movie plots and Broadway productions. (Perhaps you've heard of or seen *Joseph and the Amazing Technicolor Dreamcoat* by Andrew Lloyd Weber or DreamWorks Animations's movie *Joseph: King of Dreams?*)

Remarkably, children are attuned quite early in their lives to sense when their parents love each other or don't love each other or when only one of their parents is in love. Children understand even if their parents don't or try to put on a façade of love for their benefit. It does greatly affect their lives—their emotional, psychological, and even spiritual lives. Sometimes children see the hypocrisy in their parents' lives and relationship and choose not to trust them or anyone else. Some see love as too risky, too unpredictable, and not worth the effort. Yes, they can be told that God is love (1 John 4:8), but if or when children don't see that anywhere in their first role models of life, their parents, those words are meaningless, no matter who says them.

For those of us as family members (sisters?), sister-friends, and sistahs standing on the sidelines watching these painful kinds of scenarios play out before our eyes (sometimes with the children of our sisters and brothers), this becomes the clarion call for us to step up and intercede for our nieces and nephews, grandchildren, and children of friends to mitigate the (lasting?) damage that we so often see coming. Sometimes circumstances demand that our protective stance for the children is one of confrontation with the parent, and sometimes we must become the soft place to lean on when the "happily ever after" scenario doesn't follow the script. Yes, God's plan and design for marriage and family does alleviate a lot of this drama, but we also know what can happen when we as human beings choose to go our own way.

Half Full or Half Empty?

Leah and Rachel serve as mentors by teaching us about the effect that insecurity can have on an individual's sense of self-worth. Both sisters demonstrated their insecurities in terms of who they were as women and wives. Due to custom, tradition, and way of life, Rachel, just like Leah, believed that her self-worth was tied to the number of children she could produce. Where Leah believed that having children would be her uplift, Rachel believed that lack of children would be her downfall. Both were wrong for exactly the same reasons.

As the Bible demonstrates time after time, God decides those things that we have and don't have, become and don't become. Despite all of the odds that people may say are against us, if it's God's will that we have, we will have! It is our duty to trust, accept, and allow the Lord to do what only God can do for us and our lives. Ultimately, even this story of broken relationships and personal insecurities helps us understand that God did indeed have a master plan for these sisters, their sons, and the descendants who would become the nation of Israel.

Questions

1. Define insecurity. Make a list of your top three insecurities. Why are they insecurities?
2. Read Genesis 1:26-27 and Romans 12:2. What is God's promise about overcoming our insecurities?
3. Give examples of positive and negative competition.
4. Provide your own best definition of sisterhood. Make a list of your sisters. Send them a card, text, or email, thanking them for being your sister.
5. When it comes to men, is it possible for women not to be competitive? What do you think? Why?
6. The story of Joseph as recorded in Genesis 37 has its beginnings in this story of sisters. How does the relationship between Leah, Rachel, and Jacob affect Joseph? How does it affect the other brothers?
7. After years of watching Jacob's and Rachel's relationship, do you think Leah ever grew out of wanting Jacob's love? When in somewhat similar circumstances, can we do the same?

A Prayer for You

Father God, we lift your daughter and our sister to you for so many things: for clarity of mind, for forgiveness of sin, for guidance and direction. We ask that she cling closely to you so that as she grows she develops confidence, maturity, and competence for the work that you are preparing her to do.

Lord God, help her to avoid the pitfalls of seeing every female as a potential rival and competitor. Instead let her see them as peers, fellow daughters of God, sisters in Christ, trying to find their way in the world to the place that you have set aside for them.

Help her in her decisions of love, trust, and faith in people, particularly in men. Assure her that because you are love, you know who and when she is to love and be loved and with whom to be in love. We pray for her trust in you and your judgment for her and her future. In Jesus' name we pray. Amen.

A Prayer from You

Notes

1. Paraphrased from Irving Berlin, "Sisters," from the film *White Christmas* (1954).

5

THE DAUGHTERS OF ZELOPHEHAD

Mentors in Self-Confidence

Numbers 27:1-11

I admit it: this is one of my favorite stories of women in the Bible. Don't let its brevity fool you, because there's a lot going on here. For one thing, sometimes, despite the obstacles before you, you've just got to put your big girl panties on, stand up straight, take a deep breath, and hear the sound of your own voice speaking up for you!

Story Synopsis

In total commitment and obedience to God, Moses has ushered the Israelites from bondage in Egypt and through the wilderness on a forty-year trek that finally led them to the border of the Promised Land. In Numbers 26, in anticipation of the last big stage of the journey, Moses and the

Israelites took time out to do a census—to make a record of all the adult men, ages twenty and older, according to their tribe. This was an important process because, when the Hebrews made the transition from wilderness wanderers to Promised Land homeowners, personal property became a major concern. If they were truly going to take possession of the land that God had promised would be theirs, there needed to be a reasonably equal division of the new territory. Thus, the census laid the groundwork for revisiting questions of property rights, inheritance laws, and traditions that might or might not secure fair and equal distribution of God's blessings.

Zelophehad (Ze-LOPH-e-had) was a member of the half-tribe of Manasseh (one of Joseph's sons, born in Egypt). When Zelophehad died in the wilderness, he was the father of five daughters but no sons, which meant that he died with no immediate male heirs, who were the only heirs that counted in ancient patriarchal society. According to tradition, then, his share of the new land would be divided among his surviving brothers, and his name and legacy would be lost in the sands of the desert.

When Moses and the elders were done counting the men for the census, Zelophehad's daughters made their move. It was unheard of for them to step forward and approach the male leaders in this way. Women had no legal standing in ancient times; they were property themselves, identified only by their relationship to father or husband. But these five sisters were bold enough to make some noise when they realized what was about to happen—that their father and his family line was about to disappear in Israel.

Unlike many women in the Bible, the names of Zelophehad's daughters are recorded: Mahlah, Noah, Hoglah,

Milcah, and Tirzah. In fact, Numbers records them three times—in Numbers 26:33, Numbers 27:4, and again in Numbers 36:11. Why? My guess is probably because their boldness was a matter of precedent-setting legal record. They approached Moses and the elders with a compelling legal argument: their father had died a righteous man, not among the rebels of Korah, who had been purged from Israel, down to every last woman and child (see Numbers 16), so why should Zelophehad's name be erased—just because he didn't have sons? "Give us a possession among our father's brothers" (Numbers 27:4), the women demanded, in what may have been the first legal challenge to sexism in written history.

Apparently, Moses is convicted by their case, but it is a dramatic departure from existing tradition. So, Moses takes the matter directly to God. The Lord doesn't hesitate to render a decision in the women's favor. But it wasn't just, "Okay, let them have a little corner of land to build a sandbox for their future kids." The Lord declared, "The daughters of Zelophehad are right in what they are saying," which implies rather bluntly that the existing tradition is wrong. God went on to establish a new legal precedent, one that was far more than an exception to the rule but a decision that forever changed Jewish law. "You shall also say to the Israelites, 'If a man dies, and has no son, then you shall pass his inheritance on to his daughter.'" Because of Mahlah, Noah, Hoglah, Milcah, and Tirzah, henceforth and forever more, daughters in Israel had full rights to their family's inheritance (see Numbers 27:6-11).

Lessons for Life

Sometimes You Have to Speak for Yourself

And speak these five women did! Numbers 27:1-2 describes Mahlah, Noah, Hoglah, Milcah, and Tirzah coming forward and standing before Moses, Eleazar the priest, the leaders, and all the congregation at the entrance of the tent of meeting and speaking up for themselves. We can only imagine the late-night discussions, the arguments pro and con in preparation for these five sisters to take such a stand for themselves. They clearly understood what was at stake if the tradition went unchallenged, and the stakes could prove high and costly for not only them but for the larger tribe as well.

First, without securing a share of the land for their family, Zelophehad's name and legacy would die in the wilderness and be lost forever. Second, without recognition as his heirs, Zelophehad's daughters would be incredibly vulnerable and dependent on the kindness and generosity of their uncles for their future survival. And if a male relative didn't step up and agree to marry one of the sisters, they could run the risk of none of them getting married. At best they could possibly live and work as servants in a willing relative's home. Think about their choices and the risks that they faced. You have relatives. What happens when someone dies in your family? Yep, things can get ugly!

For the sisters, if they could make a strong enough case, one based on their father's righteous standing at his death, and convince Moses that daughters were just as worthy as sons to inherit the land and secure the future of their family line, everything would change. The land would become their bride price and would then hold such tribal value that later, the people of their tribe would worry that if the sisters married outside the tribe, the larger family of Manasseh would lose a significant part of the tribe's legacy. Thus, it would become a tribal priority to ensure not only that the daughters of Zelophehad found husbands but also that those husbands would come from within the tribe to protect tribal interests for future generations (Numbers 36).

Moses takes the matter straight to God, who agrees with the young women. "They're right," God says. "Zelophehad was a good man, so give them what they and their father deserve—their fair share of the land." My darlin', how cool is that?

Before Bungee Jumping, Test Your Rope!
Before approaching Moses and the elders, these sisters had to have done their homework. They knew what the law said and knew how the laws would affect their lives and their situation. Nowhere in the Word do we see where these young women approached Moses in high drama, crying, begging, or pleading for anything as a favor or out of pity. Nor did they ask Moses to find them husbands so that they wouldn't have to worry their pretty heads about budgets and bills. No, not these sisters! They were serious, and they had not come to play. Their approach was confident, sure, factual, and impressive. They knew they were blazing a new trail, attempting to set a new legal precedent, risking a lot even coming as women into what was essentially a court of justice where women had no voice. You've heard the expression "Go big or go home"? These five sisters weren't going home empty-handed! They would not be dismissed or ignored. Even Moses was forced to back up and say, "Wow!" These five sisters have a lot to teach us about having yourself together before making demands on folks.

Family Strengths and Weaknesses Equal Balance?

When you think of a family with that many sisters, you almost can't help but wonder about how their diverse personalities, strengths, and weaknesses managed to converge into a united front. Which sister was the shy, reserved one? Was it Mahlah? Which one put together the argument to make before Moses and those assembled? Perhaps Noah? Who was the perfect candidate to do the talking as all stood together? Tirzah or Hoglah? Who was the passionate one, the one who, if given the chance to speak, would get everybody told but might hurt their presentation and their chance for success? Maybe it was Milcah? Whoever it was, did the blunt sister realize how her strength of purpose and plain way of speaking could cause offense—and did she urge her other sister to speak for them?

One of the great things about being part of a big family, or a part of any community that functions like a family (like church), is how different people with different gifts can work together for the good of the whole group. It takes humility and discernment, trust and respect to figure out who should do what and when and why. But we can imagine how five sisters can serve as a model of how unity of purpose can achieve a common cause—survival!

Move in Faith, Always Trusting in God

The daughters of Zelophehad were seeking justice and fairness, not only from Moses and the elders but also from God. They had seen Moses handle issues of the people, and undoubtedly they understood that Moses was God's servant. He took petitions to God, who made the ultimate decision. Therefore, when the sisters approached Moses with their case, they also knew that God would decide their futures.

They came in unity and faith, in confidence and competence, trusting God, the ultimate Judge, to do right by them. Their faith and trust were rewarded. They serve as mentors to us, demonstrating what happens when we have unity, courage, and self-confidence, but especially, trust in God. Our sovereign God has the power to change centuries of law and tradition. Their father—and mother—would have been so proud!

Questions

1. After reading the story of the daughters of Zelophehad, how old do you think these five sisters were? Why?
2. When Moses brings the sisters' petition before God, what do you think God thought about them?
3. Where does self-confidence come from? Name five women whom you believe have self-confidence. How do they demonstrate self-confidence?
4. Do you have self-confidence? Why or why not?
5. Do you know the meaning of your name? Does it reflect your personality? Why or why not?

A Prayer for You

Creator God, this story of sisterhood and unity is in your Word not by accident but clearly by your design to teach your daughter about her value to you. She is precious and important to you. As in this story, when she seeks your guidance, mercy, attention, and love, she is richly rewarded. For that, God, we do thank you. Continue to show up in situations in her life so that she is ever aware of who you are and who she is in you.

Bless her with courage and boldness to speak and act with strength and authority when addressing circumstances of discrimination and injustice. Show her that you have her back and she has nothing to fear when she chooses to stand for right. In Jesus' name we pray. Amen.

A Prayer from You

6

VASHTI

A Mentor in Self-Respect

Esther 1

Despite the fact that the story of Vashti appears in the Old Testament book of Esther, upon close examination, it reads like a story out of today's headlines, the Internet, or a TV reality show. It begs the question: What is the ultimate price of fame, fortune, and self-respect?

Story Synopsis

The story begins by introducing us to the Persian king Ahasuerus (NRSV and KJV; other translations call him by his Greek name, Xerxes). Although he is the ruler of provinces from India to Ethiopia, King Ahasuerus (pronounced UH-haz-yoo-EER-us) is a toxic combination of wealth, pride, and immaturity. He is the ultimate party animal. When this guy celebrates, everybody celebrates with him—for months at a time. Then he throws a party for those who worked at the first party.

During the course of one of these parties, Ahasuerus and his boys drink way too much and begin to talk about women. As each one begins to talk about the physical assets and attributes of the ideal woman, Ahasuerus assures them that his queen, Vashti, is far and above any other woman in the kingdom. She's so fine, he boasts, that he wants them to see what he sleeps next to each night. He sends for her to come before him and his friends, but most Bible scholars agree that implicit in his demand was the expectation that she was to come wearing only the crown on her head (you read that correctly!). When Vashti hears of this command, she refuses to come and subsequently doesn't change her mind. Ahasuerus is enraged at her refusal of his command. After all, isn't she disrespectin' him in front of his boys? He calls for the legal minds of the kingdom, who tell him that because he is king and Vashti, the queen, has publicly disobeyed his command, she can be deposed—essentially divorced and dispossessed of all her titles and rights, queen no more. He does just that and kicks her out.

Not satisfied with that, the king's groupies convince him that he's done a smart thing. They tell him he is making an example of Vashti, thereby putting all of the other women of the kingdom on notice that when their man speaks, they better listen up and obey. Otherwise they could end up like Vashti! In fact, these brilliant minds advise King Ahasuerus that he should make a law declaring that every man was ruler in his own home (Esther 1:22). (Maybe you've heard the expression, "Every man is king of his own castle"? That is a paraphrase of this text.) Ahasuerus signs the decree and makes it law. His boys go home to their wives and families, probably still snickering about how the queen made a fool of their drunken king. As for Ahasuerus, after he sobers up and awakens to an empty bed, he begins to realize what he has done and begins to grieve for Vashti. And a frantic search for the next queen begins.

Lessons for Life

What Is the Price of Self-Respect?

Today's social media (YouTube, Facebook, etc.) are over-populated with videos of young people, especially young women, determined to be the next media sensation. Reality shows offer the promise of quick celebrity, no matter how personally humiliating or embarrassing to the folks back home, and thousands of young people stand in lines for days at a time for the opportunity to be the next reality train wreck of the week. (Okay, that's being a little judgmental, but you get my point.) Because reality TV tends to show people at their worst, rather than their best, many of these young people are making thousands of dollars living rather tragic lives before the cameras each and every day. For far too many, their willingness to do these things teaches us that the price of self-respect can be cheap, too cheap. Think about some of the music videos out there, each one more outrageous than the other. Are there any limits to these things?

In this Bible story, Vashti is queen and probably holds the most enviable position a woman could have in the ancient world. She had all the riches of the kingdom, servants to do her bidding, and no small amount of power over her corner of the world. But one must raise the question, in her particular situation: What does it mean to be married to someone like King Ahasuerus? We see that for Vashti, asserting a position of self-respect may have cost her the position of queen, but what exactly did she lose? In her refusal to come as Ahasuerus demanded, she must have asked herself, "If he wants me to do this, what else might he demand that I do?"

On a personal note, Susan, a former student of mine, came to visit me a few weeks ago. She spent a semester and summer completing a Study Abroad experience in South Korea. She is barely in her twenties, African American, speaks a little Japanese (which proved to be a major no-no in South Korea), and spent a great deal of time in the countryside of one of the provinces. What an oddity she became, as children in the village would come simply to look at her. Other than the images flashed on television screens and via social media, the children had never seen a black person. She told me story after story of how rap artists, pop stars, athletes (many with paternity problems), reality show cast members, and others are used in that part of the world as the definition for who and what black people are in this country. She told me that children proved open to who she was and how different she was when compared with those images. But parents of the children tended to dismiss her and attempted to disrespect and judge her based solely on those same images—so many of them negative. I was awestruck as she related how God taught her patience, grace, and humility as she learned to handle slights, insults, and sometimes subtle but most times not-so-subtle indignities. Rather than returning evil for evil, she said that she was constantly reminded of the South Korean people's source of information about people who looked like her—videos and social media.

Her initial goal in college was to pursue a career in international business and work for a Japanese company (she received three job offers), but after spending that time in South Korea, she feels that she is now being led to change her focus from business to education, now wishing to return and teach English to the children of that village. For her, trying to combat the images of young black women as lacking pride, self-respect, dignity, and self-worth has now become an unanticipated purpose and calling on her life. Her courage, strength, determination, and faith that God will protect and help her to change hearts and minds by beginning in that small village are mind-blowing. Her willingness to live devoid of so many comforts of home to take on this task is beyond inspiring. If only the folks involved in these images, participants as well as producers, could meet her. What changes might they be moved to make in so many of the questionable images of young black people in general and black women especially, shown all over the globe and accepted as gospel? She reminds all of us as women to stay mindful of the impact that our lives have on others. We are all so very proud of this young sistah and others just like her, willing to make a global difference. And Vashti? She's probably somewhere smiling!

The Impact of No

Could Vashti have anticipated the ripple effect that her courageous *no* would have on the kingdom? Obviously, it had consequences for her personally, but the men of the kingdom acted terrified that her example would set off a wifely rebellion. They wanted King Ahasuerus to respond immediately and decisively, making wives' obedience to their husbands the law of the land. In spite of the new law, how many wives in ancient Persia began to see themselves in a very different way? How many began to discover a sense of self-respect? How many wondered about the price they were paying to stay married to men who abused their power or allowed themselves to be influenced by excessive alcohol and the clamoring of equally drunken friends? How many women got the significance of the statement of self-pride and self-respect that Vashti communicated?

Beware of Party Animals!

Yes, they can be great at a party and be the center of attention. However, living with a party animal can be an entirely different story. King Ahasuerus gives us a clear look at the level of selfishness that can result from too much alcohol and too little maturity. In bragging to his friends about his wife's beauty and demanding that she parade in front of the drunken men, he sees her primarily as his property (a sexual object?) to be used and viewed with no thought of her feelings, thoughts, or wishes. In trying to gain a certain level of respect from his friends for himself, he greatly disrespects her!

Unfortunately, women didn't have much status or power in contrast with men in ancient society. (Thank God, things have improved some since then!) And while Vashti was probably a pagan, not a worshiper of the God of the Israel, she was still a woman created in God's image, a human being who is one of God's daughters. And as one of God's daughters, she is our mentor, teaching us about the priceless gift of the right to be taken seriously and respected—no matter the material costs.

With Friends Like These, Who Needs Enemies?

As the book of Esther unfolds, time after time we clearly see the weaknesses of King Ahasuerus. We see how easily he can be misled and misdirected not only by his friends but also by those who served him. We see the damage caused when immaturity overrules responsibility and when drinking to excess can be used, abused, and exploited by others for their own selfish purposes. As king, Ahasuerus is surrounded by all kinds of people: those who wish him well (his servants) as well as those who take advantage of his weaknesses (his boys, Haman). We also see what happens when women (Vashti and Esther) defy manmade rules and stand for what is right and just.

Whom do you call friends? Are they the kind of people who seek your best or your worst? Do you allow them to push you into things that are not good or positive or right? Are you a Princess Ahasuerus? Think about it.

Questions

1. Some would say that Queen Vashti gave up too much (fame, wealth, status) in refusing to come before King Ahasuerus. What do you say?
2. Does this story apply to today? How?
3. The Bible describes friendship in Proverbs 17:17. Thinking about this definition and this story, make a list of your friends. Is there anyone who should be removed from the list? Who should be added?
4. How would your friends describe you as a friend?

A Prayer for You

Father God, we pray for your daughter that she would seek your guidance and wisdom in choosing friends and relationships. You have given so many examples of qualities that are in the ideal friend. Hold her close so that she will see those qualities in others as they see them in her. Show her that you are her friend, her confidante, her protector and provider.

Stand by her and assure her that, when and if she is placed in situations challenging or belittling or questioning her sense of self-respect, she will remember the story of Vashti and trust you to provide all she will need—courage, faith, and provision. In Jesus' name we pray. Amen.

A Prayer from You

7

ESTHER

A Mentor in Purpose

Esther 2–10

The drama of Esther, beginning in Esther 1 with Queen Vashti, continues with the introduction of new characters: Esther, her Uncle Mordecai, and Haman. (If you don't know what I'm talking about, go back and read the previous chapter. No skipping with this book!)

Story Synopsis

Our story continues as King Ahasuerus has awakened from his drunken stupor only to realize that while in his inebriated state, he expelled Vashti because she chose to demonstrate self-respect rather than obey one of his commands. Apparently alone for the first time, Ahasuerus goes into an emotional tailspin. Knowing their boss, the servants get together and create a proposal for their king. They go to him and suggest that perhaps a Finishing School for Wannabe Queens could be created and the graduation ceremony would feature the selection of the next queen. Ahasuerus loves the idea (he's that kind of guy) and places his eunuch, Hegai, in charge of the school. Decrees are dispatched far and wide that all virgins are to become enrollees in this school.

One of the young women who becomes an unlikely candidate for the school is Hadassah, a Jewish girl. Orphaned very early as a child, she is raised and then adopted by her relative, Mordecai, a devout and committed Jew. The Bible isn't clear about whether Mordecai was her cousin or her uncle. He may have been an older cousin whom she called "uncle" as a more formal and respected title. As Hadassah, who is better known by her Persian name, Esther, goes into training for the possibility of becoming the next queen, Mordecai visits her on a daily basis and convinces her to do two things: keep her eyes open and her mouth closed about her background. It is during the course of one of his visits that he overhears an assassination plot being put together by a few of the king's military officers. Disturbed by what he hears, Mordecai reports the plot and saves the king's life. The officers are executed.

Meanwhile, back at the palace, King Ahasuerus is absolutely fascinated with Haman, one of his noblemen. Ahasuerus begins to lavish all kinds of praise, gifts, and assorted honors on Haman—even to the point that folks are supposed to bow down when they see Haman comin'! Pumped up by his status and the envy of all of his friends, Haman begins to notice and become angered by those in the kingdom who don't share the king's high opinion of him, notably, the Jew Mordecai. Enraged by how Mordecai disrespects him, Haman hatches a plot, not only to get rid of Mordecai but while he's at it, to get rid of all the Jews.

Haman goes to King Ahasuerus, his new best friend, explains the situation, and requests a decree to deal with those folks who need lessons on what proper respect looks like. King Ahasuerus, being the kind of guy he is about his friends, grants Haman's request, and chaos erupts in the Jewish community.

Meanwhile, back at the palace, Esther has graduated—meaning she earned the status of king's favorite and was crowned the new queen. Everybody loves and adores her, especially the king. He is so taken with her that he melts whenever he is in her presence. With Haman's murderous anti-Jewish decree now becoming law, Mordecai alerts Esther to the situation of her people and challenges her to step up and speak up via his three-step reality check (more about that later). Understanding the costs of Mordecai's reality check, Esther devises a plan of her own against Haman and sets out to make it a reality.

Esther knows from the start that her plan involves great risk in that it includes her going before the king uninvited. To just show up before the king without being summoned or invited to do so is pretty much a death sentence. She has to proceed trusting that God will protect her and that the king will continue to be so crazy about her that he will make an exception and allow it.

Lessons for Life

Who Writes This Stuff?

For those of us who are lovers of great writing and "hold on to your seat" stories, you can't beat the Bible for great literature. All great literary prizes of human design aside (the *New York Times* best seller list, the Pulitzer Prize, the Nobel Prize for literature, the poet laureates, the Tonys, Emmys, and Oscars, to name a few), nobody crafts a story like God—

nobody! Our Creator is an awesome storyteller. When you read the book of Esther (like so many other books), it has every single element of great drama—passion, intrigue, murder, beauty, gossip, revenge. As readers, we see where the story is going before the characters even get there. As a screenplay for a movie, it reads like a roller-coaster ride. Hollywood? Amateurs! This is the real stuff.

In fact, the more you read the Word of God, the more you become keenly aware of how much borrowing of plots, story lines, characterizations, and settings has come from the Word and has been used by even our greatest writers (Shakespeare, hello?). And you waste your time and money on cable TV. Girl, puhleeze!

The Odds Are Stacked Against Her

When Mordecai alerts Esther to the gravity of their people's situation, her initial reaction is fear, not only for her people but also for herself. She is clearly aware that she has less than a 50–50 chance for success as well as saving her own life by approaching the king.

She also knows that despite the fact that she is married to the king, he is a man with a lot of issues. King Ahasuerus is not an independent thinker and can be quite swayed by those around him. His friends use his weaknesses to their own advantage. As a ruler, he is naïve and immature. He accepts things at face value and never questions. He learns the hard way (the assassination plot) that everybody doesn't love him, but that doesn't change the way he moves and operates. His servants must protect him from himself. He is the original party animal and takes great pride in that title (see chapter 6). When he is drunk, his behavior is unpredictable and can lead to extremely harmful results for other people (Queen Vashti, for example). He can be impetuous, childish, and too lavish in his gifts as well as his favor. In short, Ahasuerus is a mess! And Esther must present herself to that mess, come out the victor for her people, and keep herself alive. When she comes before the king, all she has going for her is the fact that he's crazy about her (for the moment; remember Vashti?) and courage from God.

However, there is another side to Ahasuerus. In spite of all of his faults, weaknesses, and minuses (which are many), Ahasuerus does have a positive strength and plus: he never forgets a kindness. When he learns about the kindness that Mordecai showed him by unveiling the assassination plot against him, he seeks him out and rewards him.

Mordecai's Three-Point Reality Check for Esther

Again, when Mordecai approaches Esther about the decree to have all Jews killed, she is hesitant and cautious about responding. Mordecai reminds her of a few things.

First, get over yourself; you ain't all that! Yes, Esther is a beautiful young woman, but she was in a line of beautiful young women when she was chosen to be queen. In short, the finishing school where she finished head of the class was the equivalent of contestants for Miss America, Miss Universe, and Miss World combined, and all of those beautiful women made up the reject list. As for the manner in which she was selected, the next queen can be selected the same way.

Second, don't get this twisted! Remember who you are and whose you are. Mordecai further reminds Esther that she is a child of God. She is a Jew, and whatever befalls the Jews will befall her. Being queen and living in the palace in luxury will not exempt her from certain death because she can't change the fact of who she is underneath that crown. She is a Jew, and titles or crowns won't change that.

Third, it ain't about you! Mordecai reminds Esther that the issues of life and death facing the Jews are bigger than she is. Her being Jewish and queen didn't happen due to luck, accident, circumstance, coincidence, or being at the right place at the right time. No, she is where she is because of divine intervention and appointment. She is where she is "for such a time as this" (Esther 4:14)—because of who God is.

Through her story, Esther mentors us in lessons about divine appointment and divine placement. Esther doesn't become queen necessarily due to her looks or because she answered all of the questions correctly in class but because of the purpose to which God calls her. Despite her fears, she understands and accepts her purpose. She moves in confidence, determination, and in obedience to fulfill her purpose—even to death.

In 2008, our country elected its first African American president, Barack Hussein Obama. Throughout the history of these United States, generations of black folks could never imagine that they would live long enough to vote for and elect a black man to the highest office this country can offer a citizen. For most of us, there was never a doubt in our minds that he was placed in that position because of who God is. His reelection in 2012 reaffirmed the fact that God reigns. God selects, appoints, and places people where God wants them to be.

Oh, that we would live our lives in such a way that we know without a doubt that we are where we are because of who God is and what the Holy Spirit has called us to do! And just like Esther—and President Obama—we would be obedient to God's call on our lives.

Questions

1. Describe a time or situation when your presence made a difference in a situation.
2. Read Proverbs 18:12. How does this passage apply to Haman?
3. Read Matthew 20:16. How does this passage apply to Mordecai?
4. Compare and contrast King Ahasuerus's behavior in Esther 1:10-12 and Esther 7:5-10. How do you explain the difference?
5. Do you know your purpose in life? If yes, what is it? If no, what are you doing to learn what your purpose is?
6. Is this your purpose, your passion, or your calling? Is there a difference? If yes, what's the difference?

A Prayer for You

Lord God, we know that, as you called Esther to a purpose much larger than being queen, so you have called each one of us to a divine purpose. And we know that you have called your daughter to a purpose specifically designed for the gifts, talents, and abilities that you have blessed her to have. We ask, O God, that you would show her the purpose that you have gifted and empowered her to fulfill. We ask that you speak to her spirit when she is fearful, confused, or perplexed about the ways that you are preparing her for that purpose. Help her to not look at others in envy or insecurity about the kinds of things that you have called them to do. Let her not spend time comparing and contrasting but use her time wisely in service and obedience to your will and purpose for her life. Keep her safe, secure, and focused. Remind her that every purpose is important in your world because you have made all assignments. Give her joy and peace as she fulfills her purpose. In Jesus' name we pray. Amen.

A Prayer from You

8

HANNAH

A Mentor in Faith

Samuel 1–2

The book of 1 Samuel introduces us to yet another biblical story about conflict between two women sharing one man, where one woman is loved and the other is blessed with children. A word of caution before proceeding with this story: It isn't the same old tale of Sarah and Hagar or Leah and Rachel. And there is wisdom in the differences!

Story Synopsis

Hannah, the wife of Elkanah, finds herself in a desperate situation for a woman of her time and place. She is married and beloved by her husband—but she is childless. To add to her misery, Peninnah, Elkanah's other wife, has quite a few children, and she never hesitates to remind Hannah of her childless state, as if Hannah needed to be reminded.

Unlike Sarah, who offered her husband a surrogate to gain a coveted son, and unlike Rachel, who seemed to blame

Jacob for her infertile state, Hannah goes to the source of life with her grief. She goes to God in prayer.

In keeping with the annual custom of traveling to the temple at Shiloh for prayer and sacrifice, Hannah seizes the opportunity to pray for herself. On her knees in the temple court, she cries out to God for an end to her suffering. With wordless, wracking sobs, she begs God for a son and vows to return the child to God to be used in priestly service to the Lord. Her silent prayer is one of such passion and fervency that the prophet Eli notices her but mistakes her sorrow-stricken movements as those of drunkenness. He rebukes her sternly, but Hannah corrects him and explains the reasons for her great despair. Moved by her plight and by her faith, Eli is filled with compassion for her and states that not only has God heard Hannah's cry but also the Lord will bless her with a son.

In time, a son is born to Hannah and Elkanah, and they name him Samuel. After weaning him (probably around age three), Hannah returns to the temple to bring young Samuel to live with Eli and to fulfill the promise that she made to God.

Lessons for Life

In Spite of Today's Technology, Infertility Still Happens

How many times have we seen this happen to family, friends, and loved ones? A sister, cousin, daughter, niece, or friend will marry, and the couple longs for a child of their own. For whatever reason, however, conceiving proves impossible for them, even with today's technology. The couple and those who love them all ask the same question: Why? And it's a question that only God can answer. Like Hannah, we must accept God's reasons, as well as God's timing.

In my own family and circle of friends, there are women who have longed for children but have not been able to have them physically. Some choose to become mothers through foster care or adoption, but for many others, God has placed them in positions where they can have a tremendous impact on children's lives. They may become deeply involved aunties or doting godmothers. Some are in occupations (teachers, principals, social workers) where they are surrounded by children on a daily basis. God has called them to be mentors and mother figures to masses of children rather than the biological mother to a few children. It is amazing to watch the many ways those children grow up into adulthood and continue to honor and maintain ties to these mothers and mentors for years to come.

Never Doubt the Power of Prayer
Romans 12:12 (NIV) states, "Be joyful in hope, patient in affliction, faithful in prayer." Steadfast and confident in her prayers, Hannah teaches us how God listens to us and does hear our prayers. She could have explained her situation to Eli and then begged, pleaded, or implored him to take her request and petition to God for her, but she didn't. The knees that were bent were her knees, and the tears that were shed were her tears. The voice raised to God was her voice. After praying, it was Hannah who stood up, dried her tears, dusted herself off, and returned home to wait patiently and trust fully knowing that God had heard her cry and would, as the song says, "answer by and by."

The Lord has a divine plan for our lives with God's own sense of timing (Jeremiah 29:11). It is our duty and responsibility to stay faithful and trust that our Creator is being intentional in working through our circumstances and that God's plans are the best for us.

A Promise Made and Kept

Webster defines a promise as "to pledge to do, bring about, or provide." How many of us have made promises that we couldn't or wouldn't keep, for whatever reasons? How many of those have been promises that we made to God?

Hannah's story not only demonstrates God's faithfulness in keeping promises to us but also illustrates the importance of us keeping our promises to God. In Hannah's case, her faithful, constant, and consistent prayers yielded her heart's desire—a son she later dedicated to God as she had promised in her vow (1 Samuel 1:11). Think about it: Hannah had waited for years to receive her heart's greatest desire, finally receives it, and then keeps her vow to surrender the child to God's service for the rest of his life. She saw her firstborn son only once a year for the rest of her life—when the family went to Shiloh to worship.

Can you imagine how difficult that was for her to do? Yet, nothing in the Word suggests that Hannah was resentful or reluctant to release her son. We see that she was at peace, even joyful in her decision. We also see that releasing Samuel to Eli the prophet was clearly her decision, just as making the vow was her decision. Hannah's prayer as recorded in 1 Samuel 2:1-10 shows us a picture of a woman who is overjoyed at God's blessings to her and exultant at the future that God holds for her son.

The First Day of School?

Hannah's vow to bring Samuel to God also serves to mentor us as mothers about our own children's first day of school, be it daycare, kindergarten, even through college (especially college). It is that point in the lives of both parent and child that separation becomes a reality. In other words, "from umbilical cords to apron strings," those ties must be cut in order for the child to grow and develop as an individual—the person God wants him or her to become.

Again, we see Hannah fully and, faithfully releasing Samuel to his destiny as God's vessel. Maybe she shed a few tears. But she was also proud to dress Samuel in child-sized priestly robes and see him take on his role within the temple (1 Samuel 2:18).

The Rewards of Faithful Commitment

When Hannah brings Samuel to his new home to be with Eli, she is showing her commitment to the vow that she has made to God. Again, Samuel is her one and only child, the one she has prayed for, given birth to, and weaned. She has no idea as she leaves him what the impact of her vow will have, not only on herself and on the people of Israel, but also on her son, Samuel, who will serve as Israel's greatest judge and anoint the first two kings of Israel.

In 1 Samuel 2:20-21, we see that as a result of her faithfulness in keeping her vow, God blesses Hannah with more children: three sons and two daughters (take that, Peninnah!). Hannah shows us clearly that we can't begin to talk about the kinds of things that can or can't, will or won't happen in our lives. God has no limits, and time is definitely on the Lord's side. God makes all of those decisions if and when we prove ourselves faithful.

Questions

1. Read 1 Samuel 2:3. In view of Hannah's story, what do you think this verse means?

2. List three desires of your heart. What needs to happen for those desires to occur? What does God's Word say about such desires?
3. What's the difference between a "desire of the heart" and a goal?
4. List three short-term and three long-term goals. What steps must you take to reach those goals?
5. Read 1 Samuel 2:1-10. Is this a prayer or a song of praise? Is there a difference?

A Prayer for You

Lord God, we lift your daughter to you for strength and courage in the days to come when confusion and disappointment may overwhelm and overtake her faith, her courage, and her trust in you. We know that your presence is always with her, never faltering or leaving her, but, Lord, we pray that during those times, you will breathe on her to reassure her of your presence. We pray that you will send angels to lift her head and dry her tears for the situations where "why" will be the only word that will form in her spirit, her mind, her heart, and on her lips. Convince her that "why" has your name on it, and even though it might not make sense to her and to others in her life, make her aware, in ways that only you can, that all things will work together for her good as long as she never forgets who you are and what you are in her life. Show her that in time, in your time, she will be better, stronger, and wiser. In Jesus' name we pray. Amen.

A Prayer from You

9

TAMAR

A Mentor in Self-Awareness

2 Samuel 13

Despite being the greatest king of Israel and described in the Scriptures as a "man after God's own heart," David would never win any prizes for fatherhood. This story shows us just how dreadfully family situations can spin out of control and how innocent victims suffer as a result. It also creates the opportunity for reflection about a crime nearly as old as humankind that continuously needs to be addressed for women's protection, self-awareness, and self-assurance.

Story Synopsis

Amnon, firstborn of King David's many children, secretly longs for (i.e., lusts after) his half-sister, Tamar, the sister of his half-brother Absalom. Amnon is so consumed with passion for Tamar that it makes him ill to even be in her presence. A friend and cousin, Jonadab, suggests a way to help Amnon put his passions to rest. Feigning illness and requesting a meal to be cooked solely by her hand, Amnon begs their father, David, to send Tamar to care for him.

In obedience and ignorant of Amnon's true intentions, Tamar goes to his bedside. Amnon rewards her concern for his health by raping her—and then throwing her out of his home. Physically violated, socially disgraced, and emotionally demoralized, Tamar seeks shelter in the home of Absalom, her brother. When David is notified of all that has transpired, he is angry—but does nothing. While encouraging Tamar to forget what happened, Absalom vows vengeance and decides to take matters in his own hands. It takes him two years, but he succeeds in killing Amnon for what he has done to his sister. After the murder, Absalom goes on the run and eventually returns to challenge his father, David, for the kingdom. As for Tamar, Scripture says she lived the rest of her life in her brother's home, "a desolate woman."

Reads like a tacky soap opera or awful reality show, doesn't it? The Word says it's all true.

You'd think that humanity would have conquered this evil a long time ago, but sorrowfully, we are still struggling with it even today. In our society, in the military, and on so many of our college and university campuses, the crime of rape and sexual assault looms large.

In 1990, (then) Senator Joe Biden introduced the Violence Against Women Act (VAWA), the first federal law that directly held violence against women as a violation of basic civil rights and fundamental human dignity.[1] It took Congress four years to pass this law. In 2011, the U.S. Department of Education and Vice President Biden announced historic guidance to help colleges and universities "understand their obligations to prevent and respond to campus sexual assault, as well as increase federal compliance and enforcement actions." In March 2013, President Barack Obama signed a reauthorization of the VAWA. But he didn't stop there. In January 2014, he issued a presidential memorandum establishing the White House Task Force to Protect Students from Sexual Assault.[2] Despite criticism for his even taking this issue to a presidential level, it is clear that our president has a stake in this conversation. He has two daughters, one of whom will be heading to college in a year or two, but more about that later. Back to Tamar.

Lessons for Life

She Never Saw It Coming

Let's be clear: Tamar is the innocent victim here. It's not what she says, does, thinks, or wears that somehow encourages Amnon to act. This is not romantic, playing hard to get, or dealin' with a bad boy. No, it's none of those things that misrepresents the crime and devastation of rape. This is totally Amnon's sick, twisted, and perverted idea. I say that because all too often, victims of sexual assault tend to blame and second-guess their actions. Again, rape is not the fault of the victim.

Webster's dictionary defines rape as "the crime of having sexual intercourse, usually forcibly, with a person who has not consented." So, don't be fooled or further victimized by the hype that tries to diminish or sanitize different types of sexual assault by naming it something else. "It isn't rape if you know the guy." "It can't be rape if you're married/dating/living together." "It isn't rape if she is drunk." "It isn't rape if she was into it at first." "It isn't rape if she isn't badly bruised or bleeding." "It isn't rape if he used a condom." "It wasn't rape.

She was asking for it." Darlin', if a woman puts on the brakes and says no, but the guy keeps going, then it is rape!

The White House Council on Women and Girls' report entitled "Rape and Sexual Assault: A Renewed Call to Action" (January 2014), reveals that nearly one in five women (or nearly 22 million) and one in seventy-one men (almost 1.6 million) have experienced rape in their lifetimes. Most victims know their assailants. Nearly half of female survivors were raped before they were eighteen, and more than one-quarter of male survivors were raped before they were ten.

Additionally, this same report states that college students are particularly vulnerable: one in five women has been sexually assaulted while in college. Many survivors are victims of what is called incapacitated assault: they are sexually abused while drunk, under the influence of drugs, passed out, or otherwise incapacitated. Parties are quite often the site of these crimes. A 2007 study found that 58 percent of incapacitated rapes and 28 percent of forced rapes took place at a party. And campus perpetrators are often serial offenders. One study found that 7 percent of college men admitted to committing rape or attempted rape, and 63 percent of these men admitted to committing multiple offenses, averaging six rapes each.[3]

The statistics are quite daunting, and the idea of becoming a victim is depressing and scary. However, those numbers (victims and perpetrators) can be changed—one female and one male at a time. And it begins with education for everybody. In September 2014, President Obama launched the "It's on Us" campaign, which asks men and women across America to make a personal commitment to step off the sidelines and be part of the solution to end campus sexual assault.[4]

And according to the Fact Sheet for the 2013 Annual Report on Sexual Assault in the Military, more than 4,113 service members, female and male, reported being victimized by sexual assault or military sexual trauma (MST).[5] And like their college compatriots, survivors continually struggle with the aftershocks of depression, problems with alcohol and drugs, difficulties in relationships, physical health problems, and so on.[6]

The Elimination of the Amnon Mindset?

From the earliest days of human existence, women have been treated as chattel and "less than." Even today, there continues to be a universal (male) mindset (be it cultural or religious) that things should continue as they always have, yet women all over the earth, each and every day, continue to show God-given strength, courage, and perseverance to combat the evils that beset us via this mindset of male domination and control. Aren't they the building blocks and the basic foundation of violence against women?

And as women and half of this human didactic, how do we change and what can we do to change this male mindset and prerogative to deal with us as they choose? What do we do, say, or feed to our sons who nurse at our breasts and are crawling around our feet to eradicate this mindset in infancy? Is there some anti-violence vitamin that we should be taking during pregnancy so that as our sons are born, they would have been vaccinated against such thinking and behavior? What do we place within them as toddlers that will make the permanent impression that any woman and every woman is their mother, sister, cousin, aunt, and possibly in the future, their wife? As males struggle through puberty and into young manhood, what should be put in their drinking water that makes the point that the girls they go to school with, the young women they are attracted to and date, the young women in their military platoons, and the women they choose to marry and bear their own sons and daughters are someone else's daughters, sisters, and cousins? In this country we have laws, and they must be enforced, but laws don't change mindsets. If they did, Prohibition would have removed alcoholism as a reality in American culture and society, but we know what happened with that. These same laws, like VAWA, must be reauthorized year after year. These laws involve our safety as women and human beings. Why must they be reauthorized? But most important, how do we get it into the male DNA that women are God's daughters, to be cherished and protected, valued and respected? And that God holds them responsible for their actions, interactions, and behaviors with God's daughters?

The Aftershocks

The Word tells us that Tamar went to live in Absalom's home and was a desolate woman. We can only imagine Tamar's feelings of isolation and devastation. Did it ever end? The impact of rape and sexual assault can be deep, lasting, and emotionally crippling. Again, according to "Rape and Sexual Assault: A Call to Renewed Action," survivors suffer from a wide range of mental health problems including depression, anxiety, and post-traumatic stress disorder (PTSD). These victims were also almost five times more likely to have lifetime major depressive episodes than non-victims.[7]

Keep Your Wits about You

God gave you a brain, darlin', and God expects you to use it. The Lord also blessed you with instincts, a mother wit, and the Holy Spirit to guide and direct you. In *The Real Deal,* I talked about the "Love Alarm System." It's a similar system here. As you grow up and meet new people and experience new things, in your movement and moving around, pay attention to those little whispers in your spirit and those tingles along your nerve endings. Those may be the early warning signs straight from heaven to run—don't walk—away from that guy! Never allow anyone to dismiss your feelings of discomfort as paranoia, holdin' out, or playin' hard to get. When you say no, say it like you mean it, loud and mean—in fact, very loud and very mean.

Okay, I'm fussin' now, but it amazes and frightens me to hear some of the stories that I hear as a university academic advisor. It is not unusual to hear of students (of both sexes, especially first year or freshman) who pass out drunk in the middle of the street in the early hours of the morning; students waking up off campus somewhere and not knowing where they are or how they got there; females waking up feeling oddly vulnerable or violated and wondering if they've been raped or sexually molested while under the influence. The list goes on and on. Where is this craziness coming from?

Educate yourself about all of the ways that you as a young woman can protect and empower yourself as much as possible. No, this is not blaming the victim, but it is saying to stay watchful, clear-headed, and aware of your circumstances at all times. Better yet, enroll in a self-defense class. You don't need to become a martial arts expert (although it wouldn't hurt), but it's beneficial to learn of ways to defend yourself and to recognize potentially problematic situations. Investigate classes offered at your local Y, through your church, or on a local college or university campus. Many of these classes are free. Check them out and enroll! Make a pact with your girlfriends to stay aware of each other when going out socially. Hold each other accountable for your actions. Take on the "It's on Us" campaign and challenge those around you, males and females, to do the same. Boldly discuss this issue and question those in authority when these kinds of situations arise and they are slow to respond. Understand that the issue of sexual assault and violence against women isn't going away quickly or easily without a fight. Become a fighter!

So, how is Tamar a mentor for women today? Despite her brief scene in the Word, she teaches us wisdom from her own school of hard knocks. Note that she was a princess, the daughter of a king, yet her royal status didn't exempt her from being personally violated. Don't imagine that you are invulnerable to comparable risk. Even in the best of families, evil can arise.

Tamar also teaches us, as Jesus told his disciples, to be innocent as doves but wise as serpents. Remember that Tamar's rapist was someone society said she could trust—her half-brother and probably second-most-powerful man in the nation as eldest son of the king. Similarly, her father was sovereign ruler of Israel, but he was ill-equipped to handle this violence and betrayal among his own children. Tamar's would-be advocate, her brother Absalom, focused more on a long-term revenge which served his own political ambition than on caring for his devastated and desolate sister. Surround yourself with people you can trust, and then keep your eyes open and your spirit on high alert.

Yes, Tamar teaches us that an innocent victim may be victimized in more ways than one. We may not be royal princesses, but you have advantages today that Tamar lacked. Pursue education, self-awareness, and empowerment so that you don't find yourself in similar situations. That is the greatest lesson that our mentor Tamar can teach you.

Questions

1. What should have been David's response to Amnon? To Tamar? What long-term effects can these kinds of situations have on a family? On a female?
2. Standing in front of a mirror, practice saying no using different tonal inflections. What do you hear?
3. Read Genesis 34, the story of Dinah. Compare and contrast Dinah's and Tamar's stories.
4. Begin to educate yourself about self-defense. Research five resources in your community that provide these kinds of classes. Which one will you use?

A Prayer for You

Creator God, we thank you for knowing all things, past, present, and future. We thank you for being just, and we thank you for being merciful. To those who would betray and try to destroy our trust and faith in humanity, we say, "God is watching, and God knows all."

We ask for protection for your daughter, Father God, from those who would knowingly and consciously choose to use, abuse, and hurt her emotionally, physically, and even spiritually. Keep her eyes open and alert to the world so that she becomes as wise as a serpent and as innocent as a dove (based on Matthew 10:16). To the faithful, help her to show herself faithful; to the blameless, to show herself blameless; to the pure, to show herself pure; but to the devious, to

show herself shrewd (based on Psalm 18:25-26, NIV). In Jesus' name we pray. Amen.

A Prayer from You

Notes

1. http://www.whitehouse.gov/the-press-office/2014/09/07/op-ed-vice-president-biden-20th-anniversary-violence-against-women-act.
2. www.whitehouse.gov/blog/2014/01/22/renewed-call-action-end-rape-and-sexual-assault.
3. "Rape and Sexual Assault: A Renewed Call to Action," report to The White House Council on Women and Girls, January 2014, p. 14.
4. www.whitehouse.gov/blog/2014/09/19/president-obama-launches-the-it's-on-us-campaign.
5. www.sapr.mil/DOD Fiscal Year 2013 Annual Report on Sexual Assault in the Military.
6. www.mentalhealth.va.gov/docs/mst_general_factsheet.pdf; Fact Sheet on Military Sexual Trauma.
7. "Rape and Sexual Assault," p. 14.

10

JOCHEBED AND THE DAUGHTER OF PHARAOH

Mentors in Preparation

Exodus 2

This, my darlin', is the ultimate story of interracial (transra-cial) adoption! For Jochebed, the birth mother, the adoption represents safety, protection, and a secured future for her son. For Pharaoh's daughter, the adoptive mother, the adoption is all about the baby—a helpless innocent (and such a cutie!). For us, it is the wonder of how God works between women.

Story Synopsis

The setting is ancient Egypt. Joseph's reign as prime minis-ter is long past, the high regard that Egypt's ruling class had for the Israelites has disintegrated, and a new pharaoh who "knows not Joseph" is now in place. Threatened by the sheer number of Hebrews who now occupy a large region of the country, this pharaoh first enslaves them and then decides that the only way to ensure national security is to kill an entire generation of Israelite males. Pharaoh sets forth an edict, instructing midwives that, upon the birth of a male Hebrew child, they are to kill the infant immediately. Not allowing themselves to bow to this pressure, the midwives claim that Israelite women are so strong that by the time midwives arrive, the babies are already safely delivered.

One Israelite mother who seeks life for her son rather than death is Jochebed, the biological mother of Moses. Hiding him as long as she can (about three months), Jochebed is faced with the dilemma of trying to keep him alive in secret or releasing him—to what? Either way, her decision for her baby is filled with despair. Her only hope is God's will for this child. Divine intervention comes in the form of the daughter of Pharaoh.

The Word relates the story of how Jochebed places Moses in a watertight basket and sets it afloat at one of the bathing sites of Pharaoh's daughter. Finding the basket and the baby wrapped inside, she takes him and raises him as her own son, even finding an Israelite (Jochebed herself) to serve as the baby's nurse. Jochebed raises her son for the next few years and then relinquishes him to the care of his adoptive mother, Pharaoh's daughter (so sad that we've never learned her real name).

Lessons for Life

Not Just Any Egyptian, One of the Egyptians

Let's be clear here: For Jochebed, it's important that an Egyptian adopts Moses—but not just any Egyptian. It's crucial that the adoptive mother be one of the Egyptians. Jochebed wins the lottery, so to speak, when the Egyptian turns out to be the royal princess. To get to Pharaoh's daughter probably took careful planning, research, and perfect timing on Jochebed's part. It was also an incredibly risky move to make. When Jochebed placed Moses in that basket and set it in motion, she had no guarantee that her plan would work. How would Pharaoh's daughter respond to the sight of this Hebrew baby in a basket? In other words, when Jochebed sends Moses into the unknown, she can only pray (really hard) that her plan works. She can only pray to the God that she knows and believes can make her plan happen. She can only pray that Pharaoh's daughter will be all that she needs her to be (excited about a baby, any baby) and all that Jochebed can't be: safety, protector, provider, and the source of a future of peace, opportunity, and prosperity for her child. She can only hope and pray.

Such are the prayers, hopes, and dreams of millions of biological mothers every day of their lives. They hope, pray, and believe that because they, for whatever reason, can't, there is an adoptive mother who can and will.

And What about the Adoptive Mother?

Scripture teaches us very little about Pharaoh's daughter. However, although fictional, the movie classic *The Ten Commandments* (1956, directed by Cecil B. DeMille) has sought to give us a sense of the kind of person Pharaoh's daughter was. In the movie, she is depicted as childless and longing so much for a child that when she sees a helpless Hebrew baby set adrift in a basket, she immediately disregards his heritage (destined for death at birth, offspring of foreign slaves) and claims him for her own. She provides the best that Egypt can offer *her* child.

For so many women, Pharaoh's daughter represents a woman's deepest desire to achieve motherhood. For such women, transracial or transcultural adoption is no obstacle. Like Pharaoh's daughter, they don't care about roots, heritage, or the culture of the child. For them, a baby is a baby, and every baby has needs. They simply want to love, provide for, protect, and supply those needs to a child. Their hearts are strong and big enough to take on the responsibility.

Twice Blessed?

By adopting Moses, Pharaoh's daughter exposed him to the life of an Egyptian royal, but perhaps because of those years he spent with his birth family while Jochebed nursed him, Moses retained a sense of his Hebrew roots. Isn't it possible that adoption proved to be the best of both worlds for a child called Moses? Even perhaps for a child like you. If you are adopted, you are in great company! God took Moses, a child of slavery who was doomed to a life of misery and oppression, and placed him in a situation of wealth, status, opportunity, and preparation. God used both circumstances to mold and shape him into one of the greatest leaders and prophets of the Jewish people. In other words, God brought together two perfect strangers whose lives could not have been more different—separated by religion, thought, and class—and formed a bond of mutual love for this child. It is an amazing bond that only mothers (biological and adoptive) experience, and only God can make certain that it happens.

No Hoops, or Hassles to Prove Her Worthiness

In the case of Moses' adoption, Pharaoh's daughter sees baby Moses and immediately claims him as her child. She doesn't have to jump through any hoops, cut through any red tape, secure background checks, submit to interviews or home inspections, undergo credit checks, or do any of the other things that adoptive parents today must go through in order to prove their worthiness as parents. Yet think of all of the adoptive mothers who must meet that kind of criteria. It's a long and complex process for the aspiring adoptive parent to endure. In fact, adoptions can be a major lesson in human perseverance. Yet, many women endure it all in the hopes of having a child of their own.

According to the Child Welfare Information Gateway website (www.childwelfare.gov), transracial or transcultural adoption means placing a child who is of one race or ethnic group with adoptive parents of another race or ethnic group. In the United States these terms usually refer to the placement of children of color or children from another country with Caucasian adoptive parents. Intercountry adoptions accounted for 9,319 adoptions in the United States in 2011, the vast majority of them coming from China (more than 2,500, most of them girls), followed by Ethiopia, Russia, South Korea, and the Ukraine.[1] And according to the Department of Health and Humans Services, in the United States, the racial distribution of children varies by type of adoptions with children adopted from foster care most likely to be black (35 percent) and those adopted internationally mostly Asian (59 percent).[2]

All hoops, hassles, and red tape aside, that's a lot of people wishing, hoping, and enduring much to raise and love a child and become a family. Now think of all of the children who are recipients of that perseverance. They are twice blessed. If you are adopted, that includes you.

This story shows us the roles of two women who find themselves in the midst of an unusual kind of human relay race (the model for biological and adoptive mothers?). Jochebed has the lead-off position and takes Moses as far as she can and then turns him over to Pharaoh's daughter. She moves him forward by preparing him physically, educationally, and socially. She then, in so many ways, hands him over to God, the anchor leg, to prepare him spiritually and mentally for the ultimate role that Moses must play. Jochebed gives him roots and history; Pharaoh's daughter gives him the privilege of education and safety in social status. Both women serve as our mentors, teaching us about not only the preparation that motherhood provides but also God's divine design of it.

Questions

1. List the kinds of factors Jochebed had to consider when planning Moses' meeting with Pharaoh's daughter.
2. If you are adopted, what plans for greatness does God have for you? If you aren't adopted, do you know any adoptees? What issues do they face?
3. Read Ephesians 1:4-5. What does this Scripture say about adoption?
4. Read Romans 8:28. What does this passage teach us about acceptance?
5. List five ways that you have been prepared for the world by the woman (or women) who mothered you. Write a letter thanking her for preparing you.

A Prayer for You

Creator God, you and you alone know our past, present, and future. We pray that whatever your daughter's future holds, you will remind her that you are present and involved. Perhaps she is adopted and will learn about her past in terms of her parentage. Perhaps she might one day find herself as Jochebed, having to release her own child to a pharaoh's daughter, or as Pharaoh's daughter, embracing another woman's biological child as her own. Keep her mindful that all are your children and all are precious in your sight. In difficult situations and decisions, give her hope, peace, and understanding that you have promised her that she is never, ever alone. Give her courage, grace, and endurance.

And, Lord God, if she is adopted, give her courage to face whatever the reality of her beginnings were and to thank you for keeping her and intervening in her life. Teach her acceptance and to trust you and your decisions in all things. Show her Romans 8:28 in her life. In Jesus' name we pray. Amen.

A Prayer from You

Notes

1. www.adoption.state.gov.; article on "Intercountry Adoptions"; click on link to Statistics.
2. www.aspe.hhs.gov.

11

RAHAB

A Mentor in Courage

Joshua 2

As strange as it may sound, our mentor in this chapter is Rahab, a prostitute from Jericho. Yes, darlin', you read that right. She was a prostitute—and a pagan one at that. Yet she ultimately became an ancestor of Jesus, and she is mentioned in the Hall of Faith recorded in the book of Hebrews. Now with that kind of introduction and personal baggage, and if God could use her . . . what makes you think that God can't use you for God's purposes?

Story Synopsis

Moses has died, and Joshua has been appointed his successor to fulfill God's promise of continued leadership and guidance of the Israelites. Through Joshua, God is leading the people of Israel to conquer the inhabitants (there is a list of them) of the Promised Land. As they prove victorious, battle after battle, God's reputation as well as that of the

Israelites spreads near and far, to the point that their enemies practically run and hide upon seeing them coming.

The walled city of Jericho is their next destination.
Joshua appoints two spies among his soldiers to go in and
check out the city. While there, they take refuge in a local
inn owned by Rahab, a woman, who was a full-service
kind of innkeeper, if you know what I mean! Word reaches the king of Jericho that there are Israelite spies checking
out the city, and he dispatches soldiers to search for them.
One of their first stops was Rahab's inn. Because of
Rahab's business operation (which gave her intimate
access to many strange men) and location (on the city's
perimeter), the king wanted to find out what she might
know of these foreign spies. Rahab tells the soldiers that if
the men who came by her home were spies, she didn't
know it, and they have just left the city, heading that-a-
way. The soldiers leave in hot pursuit.

The truth? Rahab lied! The spies were still there, con-
cealed on her roof. After the soldiers leave, Rahab returns
to the roof to tell the spies the coast is clear and to advise
them on a safe strategy for escaping the city undetected—
by heading in the opposite direction from what she had told
the king's men. In return for her help, she also wants to ask
a favor—a big one.

She describes to the spies the reputation that their God
has earned and the fear Israel has inspired among the soldiers and people of Jericho. Knowing they are spies of the
God she had heard so much about, she had agreed to hide
them, intending to negotiate for the safety of her family
when (not if) the Israelites came to conquer the city. The
spies agree, but they warn her that when Israel's army
enters the city, all of her family must be with her at her

home and she must have the signal (a scarlet cord) in plain sight or all of them will be left behind and destroyed with the city.

Rahab agrees to their terms and then helps the spies escape through the window of her home, descending the wall of the city on a rope. In that same window, she ties a scarlet cord as the signal to her future rescuers. Then she has to wait for the Israelite army to make their move. When they do surround the city, the spies are directed to evacuate Rahab and her family first—and she is allowed to join the Israelite community as a God-fearing foreigner, ultimately marrying a Jewish man and becoming a great-great-great- (tack on a few more greats)-grandmother to Jesus.

Lessons for Life

The Importance of a Good Reputation

Joshua 2:2 describes Rahab as a harlot or a prostitute, sometimes called the world's oldest profession. Call it what you want, despite the work that she does, Rahab is obviously a woman with a great survival instinct. Due to the location of her home (built into the city wall), she is in a perfect location for business—both as an innkeeper and as a prostitute. Think about it: hers is the first house that folks see as they enter the city and the last house they see as they exit. She sees and receives all kinds of traffic going to and from the city. In other words, in her position (both geographic and vocational), she gets to the men goin' and comin'. Included in her clients are bound to be men of the military who probably frequent her house.

At some point, these men begin to talk to her as well as among themselves, and they describe, apparently in great detail, what they have seen and heard about the Israelites and the God who protects them. In fact, God's reputation is discussed so much it leaves an indelible impression on Rahab. Just based on what she hears, she becomes convinced that the God of the Israelites is the same kind of God that she wants! The question for her is how she gets to meet this God in order to receive protection for herself and her family.

How did you first learn of God? Was it from a parent or other family member or perhaps a friend? How was God described to you? What were the words that were used? And on the basis of that description, did you embrace their God as your God?

Romans 10:13-14 teaches us that the way we learn of God is by hearing, and by hearing we come to believe. It demonstrates the importance of being in the company of the saints of God as they give testimony to God's reputation as a healer, provider, leader, and friend. It reminds us of all of the reasons why we should attend worship, Bible study, and prayer meetings on a regular basis, for it is in those settings that we begin to receive a deeper understanding of the God we grow to know and love.

How's Your Name These Days?

This story also raises a second point of reputation: specifically, your reputation. Most of us go to great lengths to maintain a good name; however, in these days and times, doing that can prove difficult. With the prevalence of so much social media (Facebook, YouTube, Twitter, cell phone apps), people lose, squander, or trash reputations every day, especially of folks they don't even know.

How do you safeguard your reputation? Well, first, my darlin', be careful of what information, pictures, situations, and language that you use online. That information can be a public indication of you and your reputation. More and more colleges, universities, and employers are checking out potential students and workers via these formats. When young people are pictured drinking, dressing seductively or provocatively, and acting wild, what may be fun to you is viewed as irresponsible and unethical by folks who are making critical decisions and judgments about you and your future prospects.

Additionally, the kinds of things that are said by others about you and what you say about others (your wall on Facebook?) are also up for inspection. One piece of advice: If your mother can read and see it and would be pleased, keep it; if not, get rid of it. Above and beyond that, God sees it!

Sometimes You Just Have to Trust Folks

When Rahab and the spies first encounter each other at her house, they have very little reason to trust each other. Think about it: Rahab has heard violent military stories about the God of the spies; she knows nothing else and knows even less about the spies. She has little guarantee that they will not harm her, much less that they will keep their word and save her family before they conquer the city. The spies know nothing about Rahab, only what she tells them. When she offers to hide them, they have no guarantee that she isn't setting them up for capture. Both must show courage, take the risk, and trust each other. In both cases, it is a risk worth taking, and all get what they need: the spies escape via Rahab, and her family is saved.

The Rewards of Courage

Joshua 6 describes God's orders to Joshua for conquering the city of Jericho, orders to march around the walled city once a day for six days—just that! We don't know at what point in that process that the spies dared to enter the city to bring out Rahab and her family, but can you imagine Rahab's anxiety in the meantime? What if the spies kept her waiting until the last day? Can you imagine the stress and moments of inevitable doubt as she peered out her window, watching the Israelites marching below, wondering if day 1, day 3, day 6 would be the day of rescue for her family? What if it was not until the seventh day dawned, the day when the Israelite army was ordered to march around the city, not once but seven times, that the spies showed up? Sitting tight and waiting for that knock on the door would have taken a lot of courage and faith!

Rahab's rewards for such faith-filled courage weren't limited to the rescue of her family. No, she is one of only four women who are identified in the genealogy of Jesus found in Matthew 1—a list of forty-two generations, and Rahab is there by name. How about that! We learn that her faith, which was based on the reputation of Israel's God, results in her embracing that God and God's people. Despite her former reputation as a pagan prostitute, she experiences the security and respectability (and one hopes, the affection) of marriage and becoming mother to Boaz, who marries Ruth, the great-grandmother of David. (We'll discuss Ruth in another chapter, so stay tuned.)

Rahab is a mentor who teaches us that there are times in our lives when we must be courageous to step out in faith and trust God. The Lord can and will use anybody at any time as long as we prove willing. And that, my darlin', includes you! What a God and what a reputation.

Questions

1. In Joshua 2:8-11, Rahab describes the things that she has heard about God. What is the most important thing that she mentions? Why is that so important?
2. How do you describe God to others?
3. What does Proverbs 22:1 say about reputation? Do you agree? Why or why not?

A Prayer for You

Lord God, there will be times when your daughter will face all kinds of challenges, fears, doubts, and hardships, times when her reputation will be on the line. During those times, reassure her that she is never alone, that you are always near. In those times when she must stand alone for what is just and right, help her to understand that with you she is indeed in the majority and she need not fear. Give her clarity of mind, conviction to do what is right, and peace of mind, heart, and spirit when she does just that.

And, Lord, give her a willingness to seek out the presence of those saints whose testimonies can help her to understand who you are and what you have been in their lives. Give her a listening ear and a responsive heart that she might use those testimonies to strengthen her resolve in you. In Jesus' name we pray. Amen.

A Prayer from You

12

DEBORAH AND JAEL

Mentors in Leadership

Judges 4–5

Moses is dead; Joshua, his successor, has also died. An entire generation of Israelites has grown up under a new model of leadership, a design that Moses had initiated. The position of judge was established to mediate disputes among the tribes and to lead Israel into battle as the Lord called and empowered the judge to do so. During the history of the Israelites, fifteen people served as judges—and among them was just one woman, Deborah.

Story Synopsis

The idea behind the leadership model of a judge was that Israel would have no sovereign ruler (i.e., no king) except God. Only when needed did the Lord raise up a judge to deal with a specific crisis or challenge, whether that was an encroaching enemy army or a conflict among the tribes. Some judges proved more effective and admirable than others. Deborah proved to be one of the best.

Perhaps part of Deborah's success was rooted in her bi-vocational identity. In Deborah's leadership, the people of Israel got a two-for-one deal. She wasn't only a judge, a charismatic leader who rose up briefly to address a crisis under God's orders. She was also a prophet, a leader the Bible describes as someone to whom God speaks through dreams or visions, with a responsibility to impart information to as well as judgment on the people of God. In short, a prophet would serve as God's spokesperson and representative (Numbers 12:6-7).

Deborah is the only person identified in the Bible who served as both judge and prophet. Females in either role were few and far between. Deborah was the sole woman to serve as judge, and she was one of only four women named in the Old Testament as prophets of the Lord God. The others were Miriam (Exodus 15:20), Huldah (2 Kings 22:14), and Isaiah's wife (Isaiah 8:3).

We don't know much about Deborah's background except that she was married to a man named Lappidoth and that Israel was under her leadership (Judges 4:4). During Deborah's term as judge, Israel was suffering under the oppressive rule of Jabin, a king of Canaan. In obedience to God, Deborah sent for Barak, a noted warrior and soldier, and instructed him to go to battle to defeat Jabin. However, Barak was fearful of Sisera, an infamous soldier and warrior in Jabin's army. Deborah attempted to assure Barak that he had nothing to fear in Sisera because God had given the people the victory already. Still uncertain and unconvinced, Barak would go to war only on the condition that Deborah join him in battle.

Deborah agreed to go but warned Barak that he would not get credit for the victory; instead, a woman would get the fame

(Judges 4:9). For Barak, credit was the least of his worries. He knew of Sisera's reputation and just wanted to survive. So, Deborah and Barak went to war, and they were successful in battle.

The feared general, Sisera, managed to escape, however, and stumbled into the tent of Jael, the wife of Heber the Kenite, a small family group that had sided with Jabin. Seeing Sisera's fatigue and hunger, Jael offered to hide and feed him. As Sisera lay sleeping from exhaustion, she murdered him (Judges 4:18-22), thus becoming the woman who gets the credit for defeating Sisera.

Lessons for Life

Keep It Movin'!

When we first meet Deborah, she is a sistah with a lot going on. She is a wife to her husband, a prophet, a judge for the nation and apparently also a recognized military strategist. Talk about multitasking! Her role in the military came under protest; that part was forced on her because of Barak's fears. So what's a girl to do? Faced with certain defeat if they don't go to war, as well as disobedience to God's commands, Deborah heads to the battlefield at Barak's side.

How many of us, in our very crowded, busy, overtasked lives get called on to do even more things and take on more responsibilities? Sometimes it's the sudden and quite unexpected care of a parent or other aging family member. Or it may involve being called on to raise the children of a sibling or siblings. Perhaps there is a change in ownership or management at our workplace and new systems and procedures must be adopted or new personalities must be navigated, which may require overtime or major adjustments on our part. Or maybe new projects or programs at church now require more time and attention. In other words, how many of us are Deborahs, committed to doing so many things, yet being called on to do even more?

In Deborah's case, she realized that she had no choice. God's command to go to war had to be obeyed. She prayed and kept it movin'! She demonstrated leadership at one of the most critical times in the life of her country.

And during those times when we are called on to be Deborahs, we are answering God's call for us to step up to be leaders as well. No, it's not easy. It's sometimes quite inconvenient, often messy, tiring, and demanding, but God gives us what we need when we call on the Lord and keep it movin' as well. It's what women do, right?

So many of the additional duties and responsibilities that we are forced to take on can lead to health problems for us. The stress and mental, physical, and emotional fatigue from too many of these demands can kill us, psychologically and sometimes physically. We can become depressed or develop high blood pressure, diabetes, eating disorders (overeating, bulimia, anorexia), or certain forms of cancers, or experience insomnia. We can find ourselves taking medications or supplements for everything and anything and then taking more pills for the side effects of the first pills.

Yes, we step up and do what's needed, but we also begin to understand that we need and must demand assistance from others (siblings, spouses, children, bosses, etc.) so that the work can be accomplished and our health stays in check. Think about it: Care for others begins with self-care!

It means that we set limits and boundaries and stick to them. It means that we teach and model for others to develop this leadership lesson as well. It means that we turn off the control-freak button and allow folks to do things in their own way and not (only) our way. It means that we learn how to accept the imperfections of others. And God does give us the strength to do what needs to be done, but the Lord also gives us the courage and wisdom to say, "Yes to this, but not that" and just plain "No!" God blesses us with clarity of mind so we don't feel guilty about stuff (and folks).

We learn this lesson, not only from Deborah but also from Jael, the other woman in this story. As with Deborah, Scripture provides no physical description of Jael. She is described only as the wife of Heber the Kenite (whoever he is). We are clueless as to her age, size, or physical characteristics. The only thing we can conclude about her, based on her encounter with Sisera, is that she is politically savvy enough to recognize him—and wise enough to know that she can't physically approach or overpower him—at least, not while he's standing upright.

At Some Point, You Have to Eat and Sleep

Jael has learned the leadership lesson of getting enough nutrition and to rest well, however—so well that she can teach it to Sisera (albeit with an ulterior motive). When he shows up at her house, he is hungry and physically exhausted. She takes full advantage of both human conditions in him. She cooks for him, feeds him, and then patiently waits for him to fall asleep. She knows it has to happen eventually—and that will be her chance to make history!

Jael's actions are particularly significant because she gives us a model for action when we encounter difficult times and circumstances. We are to stay calm and focused, be patient, and move only when God says move! Her actions created victory for God's people by removing a major military stumbling block in their war effort.

Fifteen Minutes of Fame?

In many ways, watching Jael in this story is like watching a celebrity movie actor who makes a guest appearance in a television production. It is usually more than a cameo, where a highly recognizable face is spotted in a crowd scene or is given a snappy one-liner that is incidental to the plot. Rather, like a guest star, Jael enters at a critical point in the story, makes a significant contribution, and then, as quietly as she enters, she's gone. Her brief interaction with Sisera establishes a presence for her in the biblical history. It is the first and last time that we see her name. Yet, she is a mentor who teaches us that there are no small roles in God's dramas; every actor has a special and unique contribution. That includes every one of us as well.

The late, great, and infamous pop artist Andy Warhol is credited with saying, "In the future, everybody will be world-famous for fifteen minutes." In view of the way folks become overnight celebrities via social media, I guess in too many ways you could say that he's correct. Think about that the next time you watch the news or hear about someone who was at the right place at the right time and performed some act of heroism—and becomes an overnight media sensation.

Then think about those folks in our lives (perhaps even you?) who do heroic kinds of things every day, yet there are no media stories or reports. Those individuals aren't seeking nor do they want media coverage. They are being obedient to God's call for action, service, and duty. They truly are the leaders, the Deborahs and the Jaels, of this world. We praise God for them, and we thank them from the bottom of our hearts.

Deborah and Jael are mentors who show us the importance and demands of leadership. These two sistahs help us understand that God calls whomever God wants, whenever

God wants, for as long as God needs them. They remind us that, quite often, we are called out of our comfort zones to take on far more than we could ever imagine. And we are to do so without seeking fame or fortune—resisting it, in fact. We must desire to do the right thing for the Lord and for God's people. May more of us today aspire to be like Deborah and Jael!

Questions

1. Why was Barak so insistent that Deborah join him in battle? In this case, when is weakness strength and strength weakness?
2. Why do you think Deborah agreed to go? What character traits do you see in her?
3. What lessons do Deborah and Jael teach us about godly leadership?
4. Describe a time when leadership was thrust upon you.
5. Read Joshua 1:9 and Galatians 6:9. What do these passages teach us about leadership?

A Prayer for You

Lord God, give your daughter an open heart and a willing spirit to give of herself when she is given opportunities to serve, even those times when things are thrust upon her and out of her control. Place humility within her spirit so that she understands that, because you have created all things, nothing is too big or too small for her to do; all things are important to you.

Stand by her to lead and guide when she is called upon to serve as leader. Talk to her and reassure her that the words of

Romans 8:28 are true. She can do all things through you because you will strengthen her! Guide her footsteps. Remind her of the model that Jael offers: be calm, focused, patient, and then wait for your cue to move—to make a decision or carry out an action.

Reinforce her spirit when she begins to feel that her actions are unappreciated or ignored. Give her the words to ask for help particularly for her health and well-being, when responsibilities prove overwhelming and problematic. Help her to understand that she works for you and you reward all who are obedient to you. Encourage her heart to recognize that if and when she does those things, she will always be triumphant. In Jesus' name we pray. Amen.

A Prayer from You

13

RUTH AND NAOMI

Mentors in Wisdom

Ruth 1–4

At every turn of this story, Ruth teaches us about choices, commitment, and what it can mean when the young ("new school") shut up, listen, and trust the wisdom of the elderly ("old school"). And Naomi teaches us about being the kind of older and wiser leader/mentor that young women want to follow.

Story Synopsis

The book of Ruth begins at a devastating time in the life of a family. A Jewish couple, Elimelech and Naomi, must relocate to the neighboring country of Moab due to a famine. While establishing a new life in a new place, their sons, Mahlon and Chilion, meet and marry two Moabite women, Orpah and Ruth. As they begin their lives as new family units, things quickly spiral out of control. By Ruth 1:5, the husband and both sons are dead, leaving all three women as widows.

The Bible doesn't give any details of their husbands' deaths. Such details aren't necessary. What is more significant is how the fact of those deaths affected the wives left behind. Their status of being newly widowed happened at a time and in a culture that made women who suffered such losses weak and vulnerable—being left with no adult male to provide for them.

Being a realist and assessing their rather hopeless situation, Naomi urges her daughters-in-law to look out for themselves by returning to their own families and their family homes. Daughter-in-law Orpah reluctantly agrees and leaves. Ruth, however, pledges extraordinary loyalty and fidelity to Naomi (Ruth 1:16-17) and returns to Naomi's home and family, where the younger woman takes responsibility for trying to provide for their women-only household.

As a woman and a foreigner in Israel, Ruth's options are limited, so joining the other poor people in the community, she trails behind the paid workers in a local field, picking up the grain they drop or leave unpicked. In a short time, Ruth is noticed as a stranger but also as a hard worker in the fields of Boaz, a very wealthy close relative of Naomi. Boaz instructs his employees to keep an eye out for Ruth—and to drop extra grain for her.

When Ruth starts bringing home more harvest than any-one could expect, Naomi is quick to ask questions. Upon learning that the owner is a close relative, and apparently unmarried, Naomi shrewdly seizes an opportunity to help Ruth and herself.

Fully aware that Ruth is unfamiliar with certain traditions of her people, Naomi urges Ruth to create a situation where she would get Boaz's full attention. Trusting in her mother-in-law, even if she didn't fully understand, Ruth obeys Naomi's instructions. The plan works, and in time, Ruth and Boaz are married and conceive a child, a son whom they name Obed. Obed later became a father himself, and his son Jesse grew up and got married, and one of his sons was David—yes, the David who became king of Israel and ancestor of Jesus.

In short, Ruth is David's great-grandmother, and the third woman listed by name in the genealogy of our Lord and Savior, Jesus Christ (Matthew 1:1-17).

Lessons for Life

Not Backward but Forward

Although given a difficult situation (sudden and early widowhood), rather than go back to her childhood home, Ruth makes the courageous decision to move forward with Naomi. Just like Orpah, Ruth is urged to return to her family and her gods (Ruth 1:15). Naomi doesn't present it as a choice or a request but almost as a command. It's only logical; she has nothing to offer them as a poor, aging widow herself. Going home and starting over is the only sensible choice for both young women to make. Yet, Ruth chooses to do just the opposite and stays with Naomi.

The decision means that Ruth is moving far from her homeland, journeying to a strange and different land, people, traditions, culture, and religion. The only person she will know is Naomi. We have to ask, what is it about Naomi that helps Ruth to make the quick and permanent decision to follow her? For all of the horror stories and mother-in-law jokes we tend to hear in our culture, here is a woman who chooses her mother-in-law over her own family.

But perhaps Ruth knows her own family too well, and that helps her to make the conscious decision not to return to them. After all, who gets to pick members of your family? Because the Word doesn't give any hint as to why Ruth makes the decisions that she does, we can only guess at her motives. But she makes the choice and apparently never looks back. Perhaps it is her way of striving for a future with the possibility of better rather than settling for the past of just good enough.

It's Even Included in Wedding Vows

Ruth's vow to Naomi, "Intreat me not to leave thee, or to return from following after thee; for whither thou goest, I will go, and where thou lodgest, I will lodge; thy people shall be my people, and thy God my God" (Ruth 1:16, KJV), is considered by many to be the ultimate vow of fidelity. When those words are spoken during a wedding ceremony, everybody listens! Trust me, my darlin', these are not words to say casually to just anybody, for they are powerful words of commitment that should be reserved for the one God calls to be your husband—because your God must be his God.

In light of this vow of fidelity, Ruth clearly chooses the God of Naomi over the various gods of Moab. In turn, that means later she chose the God of Boaz as well. Ruth understood that going forward instead of back meant leaving everything behind. She was committed to starting fresh with a new faith, a new homeland, a new culture, a new family. Thank the Lord that she chose her new commitments wisely!

You Never Know Who's Watching

It doesn't take long for Ruth's presence to become known. For one thing, Bethlehem is a small town, and a foreign young woman working alone in the fields would have attracted attention and rumors right away. But she is a hard worker and diligent in her labor, and people soon learn that she is Naomi's daughter-in-law. So, she may be a stranger, but she earns respect from the community because of her commitment to a family matriarch. That counted for a lot back then!

All of this gains Ruth notice by those who work with her. Her reputation reaches Boaz before he sees her for the first time. Curious about what he hears of Ruth, interested in what he sees of her, and feeling responsible for a poor relative, Boaz quietly responds by making sure that Ruth and Naomi are in need of nothing.

Initially Ruth is oblivious to who Boaz really is. To her, he is an anonymous employer whose wealth and generosity are sufficient to extend to her and Naomi. She's grateful for the work and for provision, but nothing else. In short, she comes to work in the fields, does her job, doesn't complain about anything, and goes home tired but pleased with the fruit of her labor. She sounds like a mentor with a great work ethic!

When in Doubt, Be Wise Enough to Trust the Wise

When Ruth chose to go to Naomi's home, she chose to follow the older woman's lead in creating a life for them. Ruth is a stranger in a strange land. In other words, Ruth decided to trust Naomi's leadership and guidance—Naomi's wisdom—as she learned about her new home.

Age and wisdom take over when Naomi realizes that Ruth has captured the attention of Boaz. Unlike Ruth, she knows exactly who Boaz is and what he represents. What a catch Boaz would be for Ruth and her! And being at home, Naomi knows the traditions and the customs of her people. To use a sporting metaphor, Naomi knew the bait that was needed to reel Boaz in.

Ruth 3 describes the instructions that Naomi gave to Ruth in order to gain Boaz's full attention, and Ruth 4:9 shows the result of Ruth's efforts and obedience to Naomi's guidance. Say what you want, trends can come and go but wisdom never, ever goes out of style—especially when it's an older woman ("old school") advising/mentoring a younger woman ("new school") about gettin' a good man!

Launch Out into the Deep

Ruth's story is a clear example of what it can mean when we demonstrate the wisdom to have faith, trust, hope, and love especially in our God. Ruth commits to Naomi and follows Naomi into uncharted waters (a new home, new people, a new love, a new life), embracing Naomi's God as her own, always trusting and believing that things will work well for both of them. That is the same trust and belief that we must have in our God as the Lord moves us beyond our comfort zones to the deep waters of our lives (college, graduate school, new jobs, new careers, new cities, new apartments, new friends, new loves, new lives).

In Luke 5:4, Jesus approached fishermen who had been working all night but received little for their efforts. He challenged them to go out one more time, but this time to go farther than they had before. They were tired, discouraged, and ready for home and bed, but they listened to Jesus' directive. In their obedience, they went forth and were successful.

So it will be with you, my darlin'. There will be times in your life when, just like Ruth, you are faced with having to make some critical decisions about your life. The choices may very well be to return to the past, that which you have always known and done. Or the choice may be to stay where you are, keeping intact the status quo. Or you may be faced with the choice of moving forward, having no guarantees, armed with only trust and hope. When Christ calls us to launch out into the deep, to take the risk of moving forward into the future, Christ assures us that the wisdom of faith that we show in moving forward will be rewarded.

Ruth and Naomi are mentors who teach us that God is, indeed, our comfort, strength, and an ever-present constant in our daily lives (Psalm 46:1) as well as in our futures.

Questions

1. In Matthew 1:1-17, the lineage of Jesus lists several women. Ruth is one; who are the others? Why are the names of any women significant in this list? What do you know about the significance of these particular women?
2. Read Proverbs 1:7. How does this relate to Ruth's story?
3. Read Ecclesiastes 9:17 and Luke 5:1-6. How do these passages relate to the relationship between Ruth and Naomi?
4. Name five women to whom you relate in a similar way. Why these women? Write each of them a thank-you note.
5. After Ruth follows Naomi's instructions, Boaz pays her a compliment (Ruth 3:9-11). What does he tell her? What does it say about qualities that some men find attractive in women?
6. Think about and discuss the "old-school ways" of meeting men. Compare and contrast that to the "new-school ways" of meeting men. What are the advantages and disadvantages of each way?

A Prayer for You

Lord God, in your Word you give us the story of Ruth and Naomi to show us what fidelity, security, love, and trust look like when they are full and complete. You remind us again that believing in you is seeing what you can do in and with our lives. You remind us again that even though we sometimes have to endure hard times, difficult times, you never leave us or turn aside from us. No, you are always there always working things out for our best and greatest good.

In those dark times that your daughter would be fearful, doubtful, and unsure of where you are or what is happening to her, remind her of that great commitment and promise that you've made to us. Reassure her by your presence that she isn't lost but found in you; that you have her in the palm of your hand and if she calls your name, you will be quick to answer and assure. Let her feel you breathing on her as you hold her close. Guide her as she moves from one level of accomplishment to another. Have her to know that she is carrying out the plans that you made for her even before she existed, and that if she continues to hold your hand, the best is even greater than she could ever imagine. In Jesus' name we pray. Amen.

A Prayer from You

14

THE SYRO-PHOENICIAN WOMAN
A Mentor in Boldness

Matthew 15:21-28; Mark 7:24-30

The ministry of Jesus Christ is in full swing, with his repu-
tation growing as a healer, teacher, and challenger of the
Jewish establishment. During the course of his ministry, he
begins to be approached by Gentiles who have heard about
him, have great curiosity about him, and are desperate
enough to seek him out to learn for themselves if this Jesus
is all that folks are saying about him.

Story Synopsis

Sandwiched between a heated exchange with the Pharisees
and scribes (Matthew 15:1-20) and a trip to the Sea of
Galilee which will result in Jesus' feeding of the five thousand
(Matthew 15:29-39) is an appeal to Jesus by a Canaanite
woman in the district of Tyre and Sidon (in the parallel text
in Mark 7:24-30, she is called a Syro-Phoenician). The same
territory was known as Canaan to the Jews of the Hebrew

Scriptures; the modern place name, under the Roman Empire, was Phoenicia, which was part of Syria. The point in both Gospels was that the woman was a Gentile.

Desperately seeking a cure for her daughter who is possessed of a demon, this unnamed woman boisterously approaches Jesus in order to get his attention. Uncharacteristically, Jesus' initial response to the woman is to ignore her. Refusing to be ignored and defying the disciples' frustration with her persistence, the woman challenges Jesus not to disregard her just because she isn't a Jew. Instead, she says, "Even the dogs eat the crumbs that fall from their masters' table" (Matthew 15:27). In other words, her daughter needs to be healed so badly that if it means all she could hope to receive was whatever leftover blessings that might exist after Jews were blessed, then so be it. She would be grateful for the crumbs.

Jesus is so moved by her boldness and her insistence on claiming his power that he heals her daughter in that instant. She departs from him believing and trusting that what he has told her will be true when she returns home.

Lessons for Life

A Mother Does What Only a Mother Can Do

One interesting aspect of this story is that we have no idea of the exact age of the child. The Gospel of Mark indicates that she is "little" (Mark 7:25), but even that doesn't help us much. Was she an infant, a toddler, or merely prepubescent? What is clear, however, no matter the child's exact age, is that this mother lets everyone know, even Jesus, she has come for her child's healing and she's not leaving without it!

Despite the brevity of her encounter with Jesus, this story prompts a series of questions and a lot of discussion. How much had this mother endured over the years with this daughter? At what point in the child's growth and development did the first signs appear that something wasn't quite right? Was it during pregnancy or childbirth? Was it when she was slow to say her first words or take her first steps? What let this mother know that something was different about this child? Was it a life-threatening crisis or a series of little things—or maybe just a nagging feeling that wouldn't let her rest?

We might also wonder about this woman's style as a mother. Was she confrontational, a woman who wouldn't allow people to speak ill of her child? Or did she try her best to ignore and put behind her the ignorant things that were directed at her child? How many tears did she shed? How many arguments did she have with friends and family? How about her child's father? Where was he? Was he supportive or dismissive of her attempts to secure care for this child? Did he ever blame her for their daughter's problems? Did she ever blame herself?

How many doctors did she visit? How many miles did she travel? How many tests and referrals and consultations did she endure? How long did it take her to realize that her daughter's condition was beyond current medicine's ability to address, and what were the circumstances that led to that conclusion? Were there episodes of anger/fury and rage experienced at the hands of this child? Was the anger ever directed at her? To whom did she confide her fears/concerns/anxieties about her child? Could she confide that to anyone?

How did she learn about Jesus? Was it from a sister, a girl-friend, a relative, or a stranger who had been healed by him?

And what did she hear that convinced her that Jesus was her last opportunity? What gave her hope that maybe, just maybe, this Jewish rabbi could help her child when so many others couldn't?

Did she plot a strategy for approaching Christ or did she just go with the moment? Did she have a back-up plan in case she couldn't get to Jesus that day? Did she begin her approach quietly, perhaps waving to get Jesus' attention? Was she shoved aside by the crowds or by the disciples? Was it anger or fear or frustration that made her shout aloud? What gave her the guts to move out of her comfort zone, defy all political and social customs of the day, and boldly, loudly approach Jesus? What was it? An even a better question is, Do we have it within us to boldly, loudly approach Jesus for our own—as well as our children's and families'—healing? Think about it: Is this anonymous woman of ancient Syro-Phoenicia a lot like you?

Will the Action Match the Reputation?

It is clear from the woman's persistence in securing an audience with Jesus that she has heard about his reputation for healing. She is bound and determined to learn for herself if Jesus' actions will match the reputation. After her encounter with him and his assurance that her child has been healed, she still has to go home and find out for herself if it is true. Upon her return, she is not disappointed. Jesus proved not only that he is all that folks say that he is; he is all that he says he is! What do you think she told others (her testimony) about Jesus after that incredible day?

This story leads us to think about our own reputations and the ways that we are sometimes tested to protect it. Just like Christ, we are sometimes challenged to make sure that our actions reflect our reputations. And just like the Canaanite woman, we must often put our faith in God's reputation to the test, trusting that the Lord will live up to the hype and make good on the Word.

Waiting Period?

Again, in this story, there is no real indication of the age of this daughter. That lack of information begs a new set of questions: At what point did this mother realize that her daughter wasn't suffering from just any mundane childhood malady? How much evidence did she need to be convinced? And upon recognizing the problem, how long did this woman wait before seeking out Jesus? Days? Months? Years? Was she forced by finances or other circumstances to wait for Jesus to travel far north to her area of the country? Was that the trigger that moved her to pursue Jesus so boldly?

Now ask yourself: How long does it take for you to seek Jesus out for healing for yourself and your family? How much evidence do you need that you lack the power, ability, and resources to deal with your situation? What is the trigger that moves you to action?

Demonic Possession?

For a great number of us, just saying the words "demonic possession" conjures up images of movies such as *The Exorcist* (1973), television series such as *Supernatural*, or real or pseudo-documentaries about exorcisms performed by the Roman Catholic Church. Hollywood's depictions of demon-possessed people may leave most of us questioning the reality of demonic possession or if Satan and his demons exist.

The last line of one of the characters in the movie *The Usual Suspects* (1995) states, "The greatest trick the devil ever pulled was convincing the world he didn't exist." Makes you wonder, doesn't it?

It is true that biblical scholars now believe that many of the instances of "demon possession" described in the Gospels were probably cases of mental illness or epilepsy, psychiatric and neurological conditions that were not understood by the limited medical knowledge in the ancient world. Even if that is the case, what remains is the testimony of men and women, like this Canaanite mother, who brought their desperate, last-ditch hopes to Jesus. "This world can't understand my child, and no human being can help us. It's like the devil himself has taken over my child's body (or mind or spirit). Please, Jesus, help!"

Perhaps, for many of us today, demonic possession still comes bearing the diagnosis of chronic depression, mental illness in all of its forms, eating disorders, and all kinds of addictions—complex and little-understood diagnoses with no simple treatment plan and no easy prescription for healing. And for countless families, finding a cure ("exorcism"?) for family members suffering from ("possession" by) these afflictions proves financially expensive, emotionally and psychologically draining, elusive, and quite often, futile.

No wonder, then, that many people who struggle with addictions (whether to illegal drugs, prescription medications, alcohol, gambling, overeating or eating disorders) seek the help that has been found in twelve-step programs such as Alcoholics Anonymous (AA).

Alcoholics Anonymous had its beginnings in 1935 in Akron, Ohio, after a life-changing encounter between two men—Bill W. and Dr. Bob—both very successful professionals but hopeless alcoholics. Both had sought various forms of treatment, but nothing worked until they combined the practices of "a mostly nonalcoholic fellowship that emphasized universal spiritual values in daily living" and coupled it with daily contact with a fellow sufferer.[1] By 1942, the organization adopted the Serenity Prayer, written by theologian Dr. Reinhold Niebuhr.[2]

Research documents that "Twelve Step program membership is more effective than treatment in promoting long-term recovery" due to its support of a "global lifestyle change" and not simply a commitment to stay off drugs.[3] In other words, the value and power of spiritual intervention has remarkable results when dealing with the demons of addiction. Think about it: Even Jesus provided a clue to the source of real freedom from demonic possession when he stated, "This kind can come out only through prayer" (Mark 9:29).

Outside of the Box

When we meet the Canaanite woman, she has already resolved the basic dilemma that she faced. That dilemma was whether to bow to the social pressures of the day and stay in her place, hoping that maybe Christ might see her, single her out, and learn of her need—or to do any and everything to get his attention so that she might make her presence and her need known, loud and clear.

Thank God she chose Door #2! Remember: She's not being bold and boisterous just for the sake of it. She's on a mission—the healing of her child! She is oblivious to what others think, hear, or judge about her at that moment. She couldn't care less about those kinds of things. She stomps on every social, political, and cultural constraint of her day and time. Gutsy sistah, isn't she?

The Canaanite woman is our mentor in the value and importance of boldness. Yes, it may take us out of our comfort zone sometimes, but it can more often than not lead to the elimination of pain and suffering—especially when it applies to us approaching God with confidence. Are we not encouraged to "therefore approach the throne of grace with boldness, so that we may receive mercy and find grace to help in time of need" (Hebrews 4:16)?

Questions

1. When the Canaanite woman first approaches Jesus, he ignores her. Why do you think he did this?
2. Describe the kinds of obstacles and social pressures this Gentile woman faced in trying to get to Jesus, a Jewish rabbi. (Hint: Look at the disciples!)
3. What stops you from getting to Jesus? What stops you from sharing your testimony about Christ?
4. Has your reputation ever been threatened? What happened, and what did you do to protect it?
5. List five Scripture passages about boldness. What do these passages teach us about God's regard for boldness?
6. Do you believe that demons exist? Why or why not?

A Prayer for You

Father God, in the name of Jesus, your Son, we come to you, thanking you for courage, boldness, and strength. We thank you for courage to step out of our comfort zones to talk boldly about all of the kinds of wonderful things that you have done for us and in our lives. We ask your continued shower of courage and boldness on this, your daughter. Help her to stand tall and speak with conviction as she shares her testimony with others.

We thank you in advance for the opportunities that you will present to your daughter to demonstrate her strength, courage, and boldness for you as she grows, matures, and takes her place in the world. Let her not be hesitant in becoming the person that you would have her become. Reassure her during those times when she would question her ability to stand for you. Have her to know that because she is yours and you are hers, you have empowered her to serve as your personal representative to the world. In Jesus' name we pray. Amen.

A Prayer from You

Notes

1. www.aa.org.
2. www.aahistory.com.
3. www.hazelden.org, "Recent research offers compelling support for the effectiveness of Twelve Step-based treatment," by Doug Toft.

15

THE SAMARITAN WOMAN
A Mentor in Evangelism

John 4:1-30

The ministry of Jesus is in full swing. Masses of people are following his every move as he travels around, teaching and preaching and healing the sick. On a return trip to Galilee, Jesus makes the conscious decision to go through Samaria, an area of major friction and contention between Jews and Samaritans. But Jesus was never one to flinch from controversy.

Story Synopsis

The bitterness between the Jews and the Samaritans grew from a grudge match with an ancient history. According to 2 Kings 17, King Hoshea became king of the Israelites while living in Samaria. Hoshea was forced to pay tribute to the king of Assyria and the Samaritans. Eventually, Hoshea sought a better deal with the king of Egypt. The Assyrian king saw that as an act of treason. Pledging war against

Israel, he imprisoned the Jewish king and transported the Israelite people to Assyria. While there, the captive Israelites started to worship idol gods and intermarry with the people of Assyria and its neighbors. Children from these mixed marriages were never considered to be true Jews, even generations later when they returned to their homeland in Samaria (originally northern Israel).

To make matters worse between the Jews and the so-called Samaritans, when the Jews who had been exiled in Babylon were given the opportunity to return to Jerusalem to rebuild the city and the great temple, three enemies rose up in opposition to their efforts—and guess where one of those enemies was ruler? You guessed it: Samaria. Those three enemies delayed the rebuilding of the holy city and temple for about three years (Nehemiah 4:6), and the Jews never forgave the Samaritans for their intrusion. The animosity between the now distantly related groups reached an even greater level of intensity, extending to future generations.

By the time of Jesus' ministry, the hatred between Jews and Samaritans was so heated that Jews would go miles out of their way to avoid traveling through Samaria on their way from Jerusalem to Galilee. For a Jewish rabbi like Jesus to defy that tradition and the history behind it was shocking indeed. But Jesus had more in mind than just passing through. When he entered Sychar, a town in Samaria, he was hot, tired, and thirsty. It was around noon, so Jesus sat down at "Jacob's well" (John 4:6), where he was soon joined by a Samaritan woman who came to the well to draw water for her household. What began as a chance encounter with a Jewish stranger quickly developed into a life-changing event for a woman with a history of her own.

John 4 describes a lengthy dialogue between Jesus and this woman, a conversation that touches on a variety of social and theological issues that would normally have stood between a Jewish rabbi and a Samaritan woman. For one, Jesus speaks to her. For another, he asks her for a drink—from her vessel, which would have been considered unclean to him. He speaks quite knowingly about her personal history—details that a stranger shouldn't know. And he engages her in a deep theological discussion about living water, about where and how to worship God, and about the promised Messiah.

When the disciples return from their errand (they had gone into town to buy lunch, leaving Jesus outside the village), they are "astonished" to see he is speaking with a woman—and a Samaritan to boot. The woman doesn't hang around to wait for their reaction. She is practically bursting with excitement, eager to share news of her encounter with Jesus to the entire town (John 4:28-29)!

Lessons for Life

Sometimes You Have to Break a Few Eggs

The same way a few eggs have to be broken to be used, sometimes a few rules need to be broken so that we can be used. In the course of a brief encounter with this woman of Samaria, Jesus breaks a number of social, political, and cultural commandments. Not only were Jews to have nothing to do with Samaritans, but also Jewish men were to have even fewer dealings with Samaritan women. And here Jesus is, speaking to one as she goes about the day, doing her daily chores.

In his conversation with this woman, Jesus reveals an awareness of her life history that leaves her open, vulnerable, and intrigued. While traditional interpretations have attributed sexual promiscuity to the woman's current condition (living with a man who isn't her husband, after being divorced and remarried multiple times), many modern scholars have concluded that such a scenario is unlikely in that time and culture. It is probable that this woman was five times a widow, a victim of the levirate marriage tradition, by which a childless widow is given to her late husband's brother in hopes of that brother producing a son who could inherit the elder brother's property (that was the tradition that Naomi exploits to make a match between Ruth and Boaz, a close male relative).

Remember how shameful and painful it was for women in that time and culture to be infertile? (Think of Sarah, Rachel, and Hannah.) So, we can imagine how mortifying it would be for this woman to hear a stranger, and a Jewish rabbi at that, expose her deepest shame—that even after five marriages, she is still childless and reduced to living with her father or brother, a barren widow. No wonder she avoids the other women of the town by coming in the hottest part of the day to fetch water for her household!

The fact that Jesus knows her situation and still speaks to her, not disparagingly or judgmentally but quite informally, is another example of a broken custom. Such a woman would have been avoided by men, out of superstition if nothing else. But Jesus responds to socially discreet honesty with a full disclosure—and sticks around to engage her deeper questions.

Yes, It's Hot but Not as Hot as It Could Be

On this particular day, the woman comes to the well during the hottest part of the day rather than at a different, cooler time of day. Why? Perhaps it is to avoid confrontations with other women in the town, women who whisper about the black widow or who fear her infertility is contagious or who feel uncomfortable with her marginalized existence, when they themselves are happily married and raising a healthy brood of children.

It's also possible that the woman had a lengthy list of chores required that day, and noon was the earliest time she could get away from the house. In any case, let's face it: carrying water jugs (empty or full) around in the heat of the day has got to be one of the least desirable chores for a woman of any era. Having a means to avoid doing it every day would probably be worth its weight in gold. (Think of one of your least favorite chores. What would you give not to have to do it?) No wonder the woman is eager but cautious when Jesus offers her living water instead of the stagnant water drawn from the standing well.

Of course, soon she realizes that Jesus isn't talking about regular drinking water, the kind that she draws from the well, but "water gushing up to eternal life" (John 4:14). She's intrigued now and drawn toward him to learn more.

There are times in our lives when we thirst for something bigger, something greater than that which our senses can deliver or another human relationship can give us. It is that part of our hearts and spirits that longs for a relationship with God. Jesus explains that the longing is just like being thirsty for water. The same way that only water can quench human thirst as nothing else can, Jesus is the water that quenches the thirst for God.

Perhaps that idea captures her imagination because she has been struggling with a thirst for a long time—a thirst for family, for a husband who won't die and leave her alone, for a child who will love her and grow up to provide for her. When Jesus talks about living water, maybe the woman catches a glimpse of a life that won't be hollowed out by grief and solitude. Maybe she begins to understand that no man and no child can quench the thirst that only God can satisfy. But Jesus can offer the living water that will satisfy that longing! Only God can give her what she is thirsting for—love, peace, security, and hope, all of the things that we as humans need, just as we need water.

How are you trying to satisfy the thirst in your soul?

Not Judgment but Affirmation

In his conversation with this woman, Jesus presents himself as counselor and confidante. He is honest and speaks truth to her situation but never judges her. He knows her life circumstances and her past (John 4:16-18). We know enough about Jesus to know that he has no problem serving as judge and jury: we see it each and every time he and the Pharisees face off. For this woman of Samaria, however, judgment isn't required. Jesus reveals that he knows who she is—all of her, not just the polite, socially innocuous, and superficial mask one shows to a stranger but the real person with a world of pain and complicated history all tangled up inside. He acknowledges that stuff—and he extends the opportunity to have a real conversation, to develop an authentic relationship. He invites her to question him and learn what he has to offer—a different kind of life, one steeped in hope and new beginnings.

She might have been a single (again) woman with no children, living in a society that is more comfortable with couples. She might have spent years seeking the marriage and family that her culture deemed essential to establishing her as a person of worth, but Jesus' willingness to sit on a hot summer afternoon and talk about the things of God with her— a woman and a Samaritan—affirms her as a person of intelligence and spiritual depth. And those were two qualities rarely recognized or valued in a woman of that time.

In a very real sense, the gospel message entrusted to that woman allows her to become a spiritual mother to her entire community. When she rushes from that well, leaving her water jug behind, to tell the town about Jesus and to invite them to come for their own encounter with him (John 4:29-30), she delivers them into salvation and becomes the first evangelist of John's Gospel. Jesus went beyond his politically, socially, and culturally defined comfort zone to bring the message of eternal life to one considered an enemy. In turn, the woman of Samaria went beyond her social, political, and cultural comfort zone to tell her testimony to friends, neighbors, and probably a few enemies. In doing so, she becomes a mentor who teaches us about the power of what a one-on-one encounter with Jesus can do and how once one has been touched and blessed and has had thirst quenched by Jesus one must "go and tell" others. As Christians, we call that evangelism.

Questions

1. Define the word testimony. Do you think that you have one? Why or why not?
2. Doubtless, the woman of Samaria had a reputation. What do you think it was? After her encounter with Jesus, how do you think her reputation changed?
3. What do you believe this woman thirsted for? What do you thirst for?
4. How do today's social media influence our thirst?
5. What relationship do you see between the woman of Samaria and Psalm 42? Why?

A Prayer for You

Creator God, we stand in awe of all of the ways that you make the most complicated so simple. In this story of the woman of Samaria, you teach us about the wonders and limitations of water, especially the water that we are drinking that can never fill us. We thank you for being water, peace, hope, joy, and security.

We pray for your daughter as she searches for those things that will give her life meaning and fulfillment. We pray that she looks to you and you only to fill her heart and spirit, to have you quench her thirst for deeper meaning in her life. We pray that she will look to you for guidance and understanding as you grow her toward her life's purpose. Remind her that it is not the stuff of the world that will enrich her life, but you and all that you represent that raises her up each and every morning and starts her on her way. Help her to hold fast to that and you. In Jesus' name we pray. Amen.

A Prayer from You

16

THE WOMAN WITH THE ISSUE OF BLOOD

A Mentor in Determination

Mark 5:25-34; Luke 8:43-48

The New Testament Gospels are filled with stories of Jesus dealing with the needs of people on his way to addressing someone else's concern. This is one of those stories. Matthew gives it only two verses (Matthew 9:20-21) and then he is on to what he considers to be the real story. Both Mark and Luke, however, spend more time and give richer details about this unnamed woman.

Story Synopsis

Crowds following Jesus appear to be overwhelming at times, almost crushing him as well as the disciples in their zeal to touch Jesus or to be near him. People from every walk of life are seeking him out for healing, not only for themselves but for family members as well. One day Jesus is approached by a man named Jairus, one of the rulers of the synagogue, who implores Jesus to come to his home due to the impending death of his young daughter (Luke 8:41). Jesus agrees to follow him home. On his way there, a woman who has had menstrual bleeding—"an issue [flow] of blood" (KJV)—for twelve years (yes, you read that right!) sees Jesus and reaches out to touch him, believing that he can heal her. She misses the mark of touching a part of his body but gratefully settles for touching only the hem of his garment, believing that even his clothes hold healing power.

From even a touch on his clothes, Jesus feels healing power released from his body (Luke 8:46). Apparently, the release of power is so significant that it forces him to stop, turn to the crowd, and ask, "Who touched me?" Incredulous at the question, Peter looks at him and says, "Are you kidding me? Look at this crowd! And you want to know who touched you?"

Jesus is insistent and doesn't move until the woman, trembling with fear (we'll discuss why she was so fearful in a moment) comes forward, probably with the "help" of the crowd around her, and confesses her state of health, her dilemma, and her desire for healing from Jesus. He listens to her, is moved by her faith and belief in him, and blesses her for it. At that point, he continues on his way and her brief encounter with him changes her life forever.

Lessons for Life

Yep, Eve Started It All When She Had Her First Period

When we meet this woman with an issue of blood (her real name would be helpful, don't you think?), this sistah had suffered with a period for twelve years. Think about her situation and then do the math. Most of us find it difficult to handle the five to seven days of the month when most women experience our periods, yet this sistah has 4,380 days (leap years too?) under her belt! Knowing what so many of us know about what our monthly visitor does to our psyches, bodies, and emotions, it truly boggles the mind as to how she coped with this for all of those years. Face it, darlin', if you were her, wouldn't you be seeking out Jesus (or somebody) for healing too?

To make matters worse for her, she is living under the restraints of the purity laws. According to Leviticus 15:25 (NIV), "When a woman has a discharge of blood for many days at a time other than her monthly period or has a discharge that continues beyond her period she will be unclean as long as she has the discharge, just as in the days of her period."

Leviticus 15:19-33 describes in great detail the degree of uncleanness that this woman had to deal with in her daily life. Because everything and everyone who touched her or came in contact with her was considered to be unclean, she was shunned and separated from the community. Through no fault of her own, she suffered with an internal physical faucet of blood that wouldn't turn itself off.

With Mosaic Law setting the standard for what was considered to be clean and unclean, she wasn't even supposed to be around other people. She had the same status as a leper in her community. The last place she should have been was in a crowd of people. Then to try to make physical contact with a religious leader such as Jesus should have been unthinkable for one with her condition. Yet there she is, in the mix. Talk about taking an incredible risk!

Then, to make matters even worse, Jesus turns to the crowd to question who had touched him, and she is suddenly in the spotlight. Can you imagine her horror, her terror, her shame and humiliation?

Jesus Recognizes Guts When He Sees It

How this sistah learns about Jesus is a mystery to us. Suffice it to say, she heard about him, assessed her own situation, and decided that meeting Jesus was a chance—both a risk and opportunity—that she had to take. After twelve years, what did she have to lose? Mark 5:26 states that she had sought medical treatment and it had proved expensive and pointless. Instead of getting better, she got worse. For her, Jesus was a last chance, and he proved to be the right chance.

When Jesus heard this woman's explanation for touching him, he instinctively knew what was going on with her and understood the risk that she had taken in getting to him (overcoming Mosaic Law, her own doubts and fears, fear of being discovered and exposed, the crowd). Despite the fact that he didn't express it, he had to admire her courage and determination. Her action was a gutsy thing to do for a woman with her issues! The important thing for Jesus was that she took the risk and demonstrated the guts and faith to get to him.

The AIDS of Her Day?

According to AIDS.gov, on June 5, 1981, the US Centers for Disease Control and Prevention (CDC) published the Morbidity and Mortality Weekly Report describing five cases of a rare lung infection found in white gay men living in Los Angeles, California. That report touched off the nightmare that became known as Acquired Immune Deficiency Syndrome and Human Immunodeficiency Virus (AIDS/HIV).

Over the decades to come, what was considered a disease affecting only gay white men would affect women, primarily black women, in a way that no government entity could have ever predicted. This disease claimed and continues to claim the lives of countless people in our country and in our community. To publicly state or have it become known that one was infected with the AIDS virus was a stigma, a declaration of being unclean and untouchable or to have leper status, just like the sistah in this story.

In the same way that her relationships and quality of life were deeply and tragically impacted by her condition, such was the same fate of people with AIDS. People died in silence and in shame because of this disease, and many family members, friends, and acquaintances allowed those deaths to happen through fear and absolute ignorance about the risks and means of transmission.

Members of the church community found themselves caught in hypocritical and paradoxical kinds of situations due to their own fears, ignorance, paranoia, and emotional paralysis surrounding this disease. Suddenly, it didn't matter what Jesus said about visiting the sick and ailing or not judging others. The ways in which we as a nation and a faith community reacted to AIDS and responded to those with AIDS are something for which we shall have to stand before God and give an accounting.

In the years since the discovery of AIDS, much has been done via research and medicines to change the diagnosis of people dying from AIDS to those living with AIDS. Unfortunately, the disease continues to spread, with women representing a significant percentage of HIV infection (which can lead to AIDS). In fact, in 2010, the estimated rate of new HIV infections among African American women was twenty times that of white women and more than five times the rate among Hispanic/Latino women.[1]

For too many women in the black and Latina communities, AIDS came as a part of the direct relationship we have with men involved in intravenous drug usage and from men who have been incarcerated. (The massive numbers of African American and Hispanic men sent to prisons due to the country's war on drugs created an HIV epidemic spread through sex among inmates. Many of these men were released to their communities, where they built or reestablished relationships with women.) Knowing this, we must be vigilant, attentive, and yes, gutsy in order to protect and educate ourselves—and the men in our lives—about this disease and its prevention.

If we make a connection between the stigma and isolation too often experienced by people who suffer from a disease such as HIV/AIDS and the stigma and isolation experienced by this sister of Scripture, perhaps we can appreciate the raw determination it must have taken her to press through her circumstances, to defy the Levitical laws that required her marginalization, and to pursue her own healing. Perhaps you don't have quite the debilitating or humiliating condition that she had; perhaps what keeps you isolated or marginalized is a struggle with depression, with overeating, with another mental health issue or addiction. Whatever your issue is, the woman with the flow of blood has a lesson to teach you in determination.

This sistah can serve as a mentor who models the power of determination when we choose to change our lives. She had gotten to a point in her life that she got sick and tired of being sick and tired. She refused to continue to live her life in the shadow of wholeness and being a social outcast. She dared to take the risk of reaching out to Jesus for healing, trusting and believing that if she could only touch him, she would be made not only clean but whole as well. She desperately wanted a life! She moved with purpose, determination, an overdose of guts, and a super dose of faith. Like her, we have to take the risk of trusting God to heal us and to educate ourselves about that which must keep us clean, healthy, and whole.

Questions

1. What is leprosy? How does Luke 17:11-19 describe the social status of lepers?
2. What do lepers and the woman with an issue of blood have in common?
3. Do you know someone who died of AIDS or lives with HIV? How have you seen such an individual suffer from the fear and ignorance of others?
4. What modern conditions other than HIV/AIDS produce a comparable sort of social isolation for the one affected (e.g., depression, other mental health disorders, physical disabilities)?
5. In what ways might the actions of the woman with the issue of blood who touched Jesus qualify as risky behavior? Why?
6. Describe a gutsy thing that you've done. What made it gutsy?

A Prayer for You

Lord God, we lift prayers to you for your daughter. Give her courage, strength, and guts to make her yes to your will for her life as strong, bold, and courageous as her no to a world that would weaken her resolve for you. Keep her protected and secure; keep her looking, thinking, and moving forward when the times might overwhelm her. Seek out her weaknesses and doubts. Remind her often that when you see her, you see the promise of her future—what is and can be—not the negatives of her past—what was or used to be. Give her discernment and wisdom in her decisions, particularly those that will matter for the rest of her life. Draw her so close that seeking you first in all things become second nature to her.

Just as the woman with the issue of blood risked her all to seek you out for healing of her life's condition, we pray that your daughter will remember and do the same whenever conditions would suggest to her that she is down and out, hopeless and defeated. Help her to know that you bless her faith and her trust in you, even when such belief comes mixed with fear and trembling and defies some of the rules with determination and guts. In Jesus' name we pray. Amen.

A Prayer from You

Notes
1. www.cdc.gov/hiv/risk/racialethnic/aa/facts/index.html.

17

MARY, THE MOTHER OF JESUS

A Mentor in Service

Matthew 1:16-20; Luke 1:26-38

Of all of the personalities included in the Word of God, Mary probably stands alone in the scarcity of knowledge about her. But even with that, few have had as much written about her as she has. She is mysterious and familiar at the same time. She is as much a background presence as she is star of the show. She creates as many questions as she provides answers. For one, why her? Why does God choose her to bring Jesus to the world?

Story Synopsis

Luke 1:26-38 introduces us to Mary as a young woman (probably between the ages of twelve and fourteen, according to most Bible scholars) via an encounter with Gabriel, an angelic messenger sent by God. Although Luke spends a lot of time in describing this initial encounter, like the other writers of the Gospels, he provides nothing in terms of her background—her parents, siblings, or birth order in her family. We know that she lives in a small town called Nazareth. We know that she has a cousin by the name of Elizabeth who has her own set of challenges and triumphs. We also know that at the time of this encounter, Mary is engaged to a man by the name of Joseph.

Gabriel initially frightens Mary but reassures her that he is from God and explains that she has been chosen to give birth to the Son of God. Mary quickly questions the biology of such an assignment due to her status as a virgin. (She has never "known" a man, which is a biblical euphemism for the intimate knowledge that comes with sexual intercourse.) Gabriel assures her that her status is no obstacle to this mission. He explains to Mary the life's purpose of the child that she will have (Luke 1:32-33), as well as how the pregnancy and birth will happen (v. 35). Further, he lets her know that she isn't the only one who will be undertaking a unique start to motherhood. Her cousin Elizabeth, who is far too old to be getting pregnant, is already in her third month. For the task that Mary and her cousin have been called to do, "Nothing will be impossible with God" (v. 37). Mary's response to Gabriel is quick and clear: "Here am I, the servant of the Lord" (v. 38). In other words, bring it on!

Lessons for Life

Mary's Volunteerism?
Perhaps the answer to the question of why God chose Mary is found in her trusting nature and enthusiasm to volunteer for this divine purpose. One of the first things that we learn about Mary is that once she understands the nature of what will happen to her and why it will happen, she's willing to do

what is needed. Yes, she understands and accepts that the child she will bear "will be great, and will be called the Son of the Most High" (Luke 1:32). However, she's never told how the "great" part will happen. Additionally, as a Jew, Mary is never told why God picks that day and time to bring forth the Messiah. After all, the Jews had been waiting for centuries for this birth to happen, yet it doesn't happen until Mary becomes a young woman.

For Mary, perhaps it would have been enough to be a witness to the birth of the Messiah; however, she takes center stage, becoming the star in this divine production. And just as Mary volunteers, Joseph, her fiancé, stands up and matches her spirit of volunteerism. Luke lets us know that Joseph has questions and begins to doubt Mary's fidelity to him when he learns of her pregnancy. What guy wouldn't? But it takes another angelic visit to ease his worries and assure him that their mission is bigger than both of them.

Again, one has to wonder about the courage and faith it took for these two young people to answer this call of servanthood and, after committing themselves, never to look back in doubt or fear. Could you do the same? Would any of us?

Always a Mother

Scripture lets us know that from the time of Jesus' birth, Mary thinks and worries about him (Luke 2:19,51). It is almost a natural part of being a parent, especially becoming a mother—worrying and wondering about our children. Despite the huge starring role Mary plays in the birth and childhood of Jesus, as he becomes a man and begins his ministry, she becomes more of a secondary but consistent presence in his life.

We know that she and Joseph have more children (Mark 3:31) and that she is present and guides the first of Jesus' miracles (John 2:1-5). We feel her hurt and pain when she attempts to see Jesus but he refuses to see her and his siblings (Mark 3:21). She is present at the crucifixion and is the focus of one of the final actions of Christ (one of the seven last words). First, he saves one of the thieves crucified with him; then he gives John, the "beloved disciple," the responsibility for her care.

Finally, the last time we encounter Mary is after the ascension of Christ into heaven. She is present in the upper room with the disciples and other women who have come together to "devote themselves to prayer" (Acts 1:14). We know nothing of how much longer she lives or when she dies. It is as if she ends this drama in the same way that she begins it, with little known about her.

We learn from Mary that despite our best efforts, it is next to impossible to safeguard and protect our children forever. As mothers, we must let our children go (even your mother had to release you) to find their own purpose and life's destination (their own Jeremiah 29:11). As Mary did, we stand on the sidelines and pray—hard.

Growing Up and Out

Over time and as Jesus grows into adulthood, Mary becomes a mentor for us as women and mothers, teaching us what it means to have children grow up in and then grow out of our arms in order for them to grow to their full potential for the work and purpose that God calls them to do. Mary reminds us that God does indeed give everyone a purpose and a specific work to do in life (see Jeremiah 29:11). Often it's not the glamorous stuff of fame and fortune (no *People* magazine covers or for-the-moment social media phenoms) but the kinds of things that are background, needed, and most important; the kinds of things that are quiet, dutiful, and honor God.

The 2004 movie *The Passion of the Christ* (great movie!) shows us a Mary who is easily identifiable as a loving and concerned mother but who is often overwhelmed and confused at the things said and done about her son, Jesus. She is just as shocked and surprised at many of his miracles, healings, and ministry as we are as observers. In fact, she is watching Jesus just like we are! It is clear that she signed up for this mission but was clueless as to what it really means to give birth to the Son of God. How could she have known? She stands as an example to mothers who question the life's work that our children are sometimes called to do but leaves us troubled, confused, and worried.

Mary's Song

After Gabriel appears to Mary and announces that her cousin Elizabeth is expecting a child, the newly pregnant Mary goes to visit her. Scripture states that as Mary enters the room to greet Elizabeth, the baby that Elizabeth is carrying leaps within her womb.

These women are not just cousins but sisters now bound together by dual divine purpose. Both women rejoice together, and Mary speaks what is known as her song, or The Magnificat (Luke 1:46-55). This statement of joy, adoration, and praise gives glory and honor to God for looking upon her with favor in spite of who she is in life ("the lowliness of his servant") and for all that God has done for Israel. It is a testament to the fact that when God calls people for divine purposes, God truly can call anybody—no matter who they are, where they are, or what they do. God empowers regardless of what we feel are our own limitations, weaknesses, or strengths.

The Rewards of Humility

Mary's song also gives us an indication of the kind of person she is. She shows us her humility as she identifies herself as a lowly servant of God (Luke 1:48). Perhaps this is another factor in her selection as the mother of Christ?

Let's be honest here, we live in a culture that sends extremely mixed messages about virtues like humility. On one hand, humility doesn't win a lot of points. Today's media in all forms often promote the opposite. People are encouraged to publish, publicize, and expose as much about their lives as possible: the good and the bad—and the uglier, the better! Being shy, private, or secretive no longer gets you anywhere. In too many cases, folks get rewarded for their extreme displays of behavior with television shows and recording contracts.

The opposite of that is apparently there is so little humility in the culture, it has become so rare and such an oddity that people can quickly become overnight media sensations when they are seen demonstrating it. Think about it: How often do we see in today's media people being elevated to hero status (famous for fifteen minutes) for doing simple, honest things? Situations like finding and returning money, animals, or objects can get you on the 6 o'clock news as the lead-in story! Or you can show a kindness to someone and get a million hits on YouTube. Is this the definition of humility that God honors? Would Mary's song be a hit on YouTube?

Last, Mary's song is a statement of her place in the future history of God's people. Because of her willingness to be obedient, she is thrilled, overwhelmed, and humbled "that generations will call me blessed" (Luke 1:48). And we continue to do so as we annually watch/celebrate her as she gives birth to the baby, Jesus (2:1-20).

Perhaps the greatest lesson that Mary mentors for us is that God calls people into service for God's purposes regardless of our assessment of our own strengths, weaknesses, abilities, or capabilities. The Lord especially loves us to demonstrate humility, for it is the virtue modeled for human beings by Christ. Just as Mary quickly and enthusiastically said yes to God's call to servanthood, let us do likewise.

Questions

1. Why do you think God would call a young woman like Mary to carry out this divine assignment? Does God still call the young? Why?
2. Read 1 Timothy 4:12. How does God instruct the young?
3. Read Philippians 2:5-11. How is humility described?
4. Why is humility so important to God? Find three other Scriptures about humility.
5. Give three examples of how our society praises and criticizes humility. Why the ambivalence?

A Prayer for You

Creator God, how blessed we are to know that there are no age restrictions or limitations when you call us into your divine service. Time after time you show us in your Word that you can call anyone at any time to do anything that you would have us do. Thank you for thinking of us as your hands, your feet, and your voice when you call us.

As you call your daughter to the work that you have assigned to her hands, talents, skills, and abilities, give her the courage to say yes and to come to your work with Mary's enthusiasm and the humility of Christ. Help her to understand that she works for you regardless of where she works. Place in her spirit a work ethic that reflects you. Teach her to stay focused, interested, and alert in her duties. Reassure her of your presence when she might doubt, falter, or complain. Remind her that she is yours and you are her strength. In Jesus' name we pray. Amen.

A Prayer from You

18

MARY MAGDALENE
A Mentor in Steadfastness

Matthew 27:56-61; Mark 16:9; Luke 8:2; John 20:1-20

Through thick and thin, she's there. Her presence is constant, consistent, and unwavering in the records of all of the Gospels, where she is mentioned fourteen times. Once Mary Magdalene appears on the biblical stage, she never leaves until the final curtain goes down. Despite all that we know of her attention to Christ, we know little about her personal life. Who is she and what drives her loyalty?

Story Synopsis

Early in Jesus' ministry, he calls the twelve who will become his disciples and begins to move around from town to town healing the sick and deranged and performing miracles in addition to preaching. One of his specialties is the power to identify demonic possession in people and cast the demons out of their human hosts. According to the Gospels of Mark (16:9) and Luke (8:2), in the course of moving around and performing this kind of work, Jesus meets and heals Mary Magdalene of seven demons. Once delivered, Mary becomes a female disciple of Christ in that she never leaves him and she follows him as do all of the male disciples.

Mary's name is associated with Magdala, a thriving, populous town on the coast of Galilee about three miles from Capernaum. It may have been her birthplace. Further, it is speculated that Mary Magdalene may have been involved in some way in the dye works and textile industries of Magdala, which might explain her financial ability to help Jesus and the disciples (Luke 8:1-3). The Word gives no indication of family life (parents, siblings, marital status, children, etc.). For all practical purposes, she seems to be a free and independent woman who makes the conscious decision to leave everything and everyone she knows and loves to follow Christ, whom she obviously loves more than anything.

Lessons for Life

Specialist and Expert Diagnostician

As one reads the accounts in the Gospels of Jesus' ministry, we find that one of the reasons for the growth of his reputation as a healer is his ability to recognize and cast out demons. Time after time, he is sought out to deal with evil spirits in young and old, male and female. In other words, he signifies freedom from the control and oppression of demonic possession. Desperate for relief, folks like Mary Magdalene hear about him in some form or fashion, search for him, find him, and are not disappointed.

In fact, Jesus is so good at this kind of work that the Pharisees accuse him of being a devil or demon (Matthew 9:34; John 8:48-52; as in it takes one to know one?). In spite of negativity from the powers that be, Jesus continues to deliver people from these afflictions.

Demons Then, Mental Illness Now?

The Gospel of Luke informs us that Mary didn't come alone in seeking healing from Jesus (8:2). She was joined by other women seeking the same kind of relief; however, Mary's affliction was apparently the worst of the group because Luke specifically states that she had "seven demons."

Well, one of the things that we have to ask ourselves, due to the personal kinds of torture that demonic possession inflicted on its victims in Jesus' time, are we seeing similar afflictions via mental illness now? The National Alliance on Mental Illness (NAMI) defines mental illness as a medical condition that disrupts a person's thinking, feeling, mood, and ability to relate to others and daily functioning (www.nami.org). Further, the National Institute of Mental Health (NIMH) states that the top eight mental illnesses that tend to affect women the most are anxiety disorders, attention deficit hyperactivity disorder (ADHD), bipolar disorder, borderline personality disorder, depression, postpartum depression, eating disorders, and schizophrenia (www.nimh.nih.gov). Could Mary have been afflicted by any or all of these?

The National Alliance of Mental Illness states:

■ 1 in 4 adults experience mental illness in a given year; 1 in 17 live with a serious mental illness.

■ African American and Hispanic Americans used mental health services at about one-half the rate of whites in the past year and Asian Americans at about one-third the rate.

■ Adults living with serious mental illness die on average twenty-five years earlier than other Americans.

■ One-half of all chronic mental illness begins by age fourteen, three-quarters by age twenty-four.

■ Suicide is the third leading cause of death for persons aged fifteen to twenty-four years; more than 90 percent of those who die by suicide had one or more mental disorders.[1]

Think about it: How many times has our nation experienced periods of national mourning due to the senseless violence perpetrated by some mentally deranged (demon possessed?) gunman? What about the numbers of shootings that don't make the national news but become the lead stories of our local 6 o'clock news? What does this say about our nation, its gun laws, and its acknowledgment about the mentally ill among us? What does it say about our families, friends, or colleagues whom we see experiencing difficulty in coping? What does it say about us and the way that we are handling or not handling our own emotional, psychological, or stress-induced difficulties? What must happen for us to learn that education, professional support, and calling on Jesus (just like Mary Magdalene and the other sistahs with her) are the keys to our freedom from this kind of bondage?

Mary Magdalene teaches us the dangers of trying to heal ourselves from the afflictions (demons, mental illnesses, disorders, addictions) that afflict us. She models for us what the awesome healing power of God can do in our lives if we but seek Christ and ask for healing—no matter what the affliction might be!

Purpose-Driven

The Word is clear that after Mary Magdalene receives healing and freedom from the seven demons she becomes a committed disciple of Jesus. She is there with the Twelve (Luke

8:1-2) to support him in every way that she can. In other words, her sole purpose in life becomes Christ as we see her unwavering presence through good times and the really difficult times in his ministry. She stands at the cross during the crucifixion and helps in laying Jesus' body to rest in the tomb; she is the first person to come to the tomb, the first to see and speak to Jesus at the resurrection, and the first to speak to the disciples about the risen Jesus (John 20:1-20). She is a solid presence in the Word of God. In terms of relationship to Jesus Christ, no other woman, other than his mother, holds as much regard as Mary Magdalene.

Perhaps the greatest lesson that Mary Magdalene gives to us is a phenomenal example of loyalty and devotion to Christ. True, we know little about her personal background, but this we do know: while many people returned to their homes, lives, and circumstances after being healed by Jesus for all manner of maladies, Mary of Magdala remained, and as a result, she becomes a mentor who teaches us the beauty of steadfastness. When she follows Jesus, she is totally committed. She knows the freedom that Jesus gives her in removing the demons from her life; she has no intention of going back but every intention of moving forward with him. Her loyalty and devotion to Christ allow her a ringside seat and an eyewitness account of his every move. She shows us that in healing, God creates a new beginning, a new purpose, and a new life for us in Jesus.

Questions

1. Why do you think Mary Magdalene follows Jesus?
2. Other than loyalty and devotion to Jesus, what other character traits does Mary Magdalene exhibit?

3. In view of her relationship to Jesus, how do you think Mary Magdalene spent her later years?

4. In many cases, after Jesus healed people, he instructed them to return to their homes. Either he didn't do that with Mary Magdalene—or she refused to listen to him. What other sister of Scripture does that remind you of? Why do you think Jesus allowed Mary Magdalene and the other women to follow him as disciples?

A Prayer for You

Lord God, just as Mary Magdalene sought your healing power in her life and was rewarded, in those times when healing power is needed, touch your daughter. Help her to understand that there is freedom in you: freedom from the oppressive hold of sin, freedom to pursue the life that you would have her lead, and freedom from her own doubts and fears.

And, as Mary Magdalene proved loyal and steadfast to Christ, give your daughter wisdom to be just as steadfast and loyal to you, your grace, and your mercy. Teach her the value of faithfulness as she grows into womanhood. And when times get rough, hold her steady and secure. Help her to feel you as you hold her in the hollow of your hand. In Jesus' name we pray. Amen.

A Prayer from You

Notes

1. www.nami.org/factsheets/mentalillness_factsheet.pdf.

19

EUNICE AND LOIS

Mentors in Faithfulness

2 Timothy 1:5

During the course of the Apostle Paul's four missionary journeys, the city of Lystra proved to be one of great significance for him. Paul was almost declared a saint there because he healed a man who had been lame since birth; he was almost stoned to death there, established a church, and at some point in that history met Eunice and Lois, two women of remarkable faith.

Story Synopsis

The Bible reveals very little about Eunice and Lois, but what it does tell us speaks volumes. We know that when Paul met them, they were living in Lystra, a city located in the eastern part of Lycaonia (bounded on the north by Galatia). We know that Lois was the mother of Eunice, and Eunice had a young adult son named Timothy. Because we know that Timothy was the product of a mixed marriage, we may conclude that Eunice, a Jewish woman, was married to a Greek man, Timothy's father. We also know that Eunice became a widow, a single mother raising her son with the support of her own aging mother.

We know that Lois, Eunice's mother, is the first and only woman in the Bible to be called "grandmother" (2 Timothy 1:5). And most important, we know that these two women raised Timothy in a godly way. The Apostle Paul pays these two women the greatest compliment in that he reminds Timothy that "from childhood you have known the sacred writings," having been steeped in Scripture by his grandmother Lois and mother, Eunice (2 Timothy 3:15).

The books of First and Second Timothy are letters attributed to Paul, writing to Timothy, who has grown into young adulthood and has become a minister. These letters express a love, respect, and regard for a young man whom Paul calls "my loyal child in the faith" (1 Timothy 1:2). We can only imagine the affection and gratitude that Eunice and Lois must have felt for Paul as he took Timothy under his wings and embraced him as a "beloved child" (2 Timothy 1:2). How God must have answered their prayers by providing such a spiritual father for this son.

Lessons for Life

Setting the Right Foundation

In many ways, Eunice and Lois were faced with an issue that many women are facing today: How does a single mom raise a son to be a man? Our culture brims over with conflicting statistics, advice, and suggestions about all the ways that women must and must not, should and shouldn't, can and can't attempt to bridge the gap from childhood to adulthood for their beloved man-child. And that's before the child even takes his first steps outside of the home and becomes vulnerable to outside influences! We can only guess at the questions these two women asked themselves as they tried their best to be mother and father to Timothy.

And remember that Timothy was the offspring of a culturally and religiously mixed marriage (Greek dad, Jewish mom). We can imagine how those cultural differences might have created tensions in the household as Eunice, with her mother's support, worked to raise her son in the Jewish faith while Timothy's father (and other family members perhaps?) undoubtedly had expectations about what it meant to raise a Greek man.

Scripture lets us know that a woman's first responsibility, even when raising a child without a present and involved father, is to be obedient to Deuteronomy 11:18-19. There we, as God's people, are admonished to teach the Word of God to our children. That's monumental in importance because this responsibility is not delegated to any other authority (not schools, organizations, clubs, etc.) outside of the home and family. As parents, we are given the responsibility (and God holds us accountable) for the religious instruction of our children.

Based on Paul's affirmation of Timothy, we can presume that Eunice and Lois must have begun to practice the principles of Deuteronomy 11:18-19 from the start. The New International Version translates 2 Timothy 3:15 as "from infancy you have known the Holy Scriptures." From infancy! Think about that for a minute: Before the child is even verbal, before he is literate enough to read a word of the Word for himself, Eunice and Lois were covering him in the Word of God. How powerful a beginning is that! Women and mothers, take note.

Mentor Qualifications

We can only imagine the prayers said by Eunice and Lois for God to send a mentor who would prove to be a worthy friend, guide, and positive influence for Timothy so that he might learn not only what it means to be a man but also how to be a man of God.

How many of us as mothers are doing the same? How many of us read the newspapers, watch the evening news, check out the 24/7 news feeds online, get headlines sent to our smart phones, or just look around at our communities and realize that to be young and male—especially if that young man is also black or Hispanic—can prove to be a deadly combination? How many of us are observing and considering carefully the men at church or in the community, male teachers and coaches, and our own male family members—assessing them as potential mentors for our sons? Men who can and will teach our young males (black and Hispanic males present a particular need) not only how to become men in America but specifically godly young men? How many of us are asking for God's guidance and direction while we conduct our mentor search? Better yet, how many of us, like Eunice and Lois, are asking God to make the selection and send a mentor for our sons?

God not only heard and answered Eunice's and Lois's prayers, but they hit the divine jackpot. God provided the apostle Paul, who took on the task with enthusiasm, excitement, devotion, and passion. Talk about a suitable mentor! Building on Eunice's and Lois's early work of making sure that Timothy had a solid foundation in the Scriptures, Paul didn't have to spend time converting, convincing, or coaxing Timothy concerning who God is. Paul could begin the work of mentoring Timothy in the work of the Lord right away, teaching him about how to take responsibility for his own shortcomings, encouraging him to act confidently in his gifts even as a young adult, and challenging him to establish a standard of personal integrity in his interactions with other people. In turn, God blessed Paul with the love and devotion of a spiritual son. That's a pretty good mentoring match— pairing an apparently single man without children and a young man in need of a father figure. What an answer to prayer for the mother and grandmother who were faithful in their efforts to raise a godly young man in the fear and knowledge of the Lord. God created a win-win-win situation for all involved.

Perhaps the greatest lesson that our mentors Eunice and Lois teach us is that, in the years they had to nurture and influence Timothy, they provided the best possible foundation within Timothy—faithfully saturating his mind and spirit in the Word of God. Whether you are a parent already or looking forward to a future when you have the privilege and responsibility of nurturing and mentoring children, you will daily realize that the childhood years are fleeting; they don't offer a lot of time to say or do everything to prepare young people for the world in which they have to live. Remembering the example of Eunice and Lois, we can imitate them by establishing within the children entrusted to our care a similar foundation of faithfulness, grounded in the Word of God. And pray—like crazy!

Questions

1. How do culture and society define manhood? What about black or Hispanic manhood? What do you think are the origins of those definitions?

2. How do culture and society define womanhood, and what are those origins?

3. What impact do these definitions of manhood and womanhood have on women today?

4. How can a thorough knowledge of Scripture offer young men and women today a better foundation for creating a godly definition of manhood and womanhood?

5. What woman in your life has served as a Eunice or Lois, a spiritual mother or grandmother who models faithfulness and godliness and who has made it a priority to give you a strong foundation in Bible knowledge? Send her a card telling her of your appreciation for the ways in which she has mentored and nurtured you.

A Prayer for You

Lord God, we look to you for all that your daughter needs and for the situations in which she may find herself in the future. Reassure her, as you surely did Eunice and Lois, that you are aware of where she is and what is happening to her and that you've already provided the solution.

We pray for her future. Let her not be worried or overly concerned at its pace. You control time, and you alone know when all that you have for her will be the right time and the right conditions. We pray for her security, her provision, and the work that you have assigned to her. Just as Paul proved to be an invaluable mentor for Timothy when needed, so provide a similar mentor for her—male or female. And whenever possible, allow your daughter to be the same for a child or young person who might need her.

Help her to be an example of you for everyone she meets. Just as Paul encouraged Timothy to stand strong especially in his youth, help her to do the same. Help her to be confident and competent. Keep her focused and on the right path, the path to you. In Jesus' name we pray. Amen.

A Prayer from You

20

LYDIA

A Mentor in Hospitality and Generosity

Acts 16

Lydia is a rarity in Scripture: a single, financially independent, and free-thinking woman. She stands out among the women the Apostle Paul meets on his missionary journeys. She becomes a friend, a committed convert to the faith, and a financial support. Her home becomes a place of refuge for Paul and Silas and the birthplace of the church at Philippi. In short, this sistah is the real deal—smart, savvy in business, known and respected in her community, and loves the Lord.

Story Synopsis

The Apostle Paul came to the city of Philippi during his second missionary journey. Philippi was a leading city of the district of Macedonia and a Roman colony (Acts 16:12). On a Sabbath, Paul and Silas went to the river for prayer and encountered a group of women gathered there to do the same. Lydia was among the group.

Scripture tells us that Lydia was a woman of Philippi and a tradesperson in the purple dye industry. Biblical scholars have debated exactly who she was and where she came from. Tradition holds that she was probably a native of Thyatira, another city in the region and one that was known for its craft and trade guilds and renowned for its dyers and their dying process. It was believed that no other place could produce the scarlet and purple cloth that the rich and the not-so-rich sought to possess for clothing, accessories, and ornamental embellishments. The manufacture and trade of these products proved to be a lucrative endeavor.

So, what we do know about Lydia is that she was probably a woman of independent means. No man's name is even associated with her, so she probably was the heir of a wealthy father or was a well-to-do widow who had no reason to remarry. She was head of her household, and when she responded to the gospel presented by Paul and Silas, her entire household was baptized with her. She was a leader in the community and became leader of the first house church in Philippi.

Lessons for Life

Curious by Nature?

Scripture offers nothing about Lydia's origins or how she came to be among the small community of women who gathered weekly for worship in Philippi. While it seems unlikely that she was Jewish, it is possible that she was a God-fearing Gentile. Some scholars have speculated that the gathering of women at the river was an alternative for a community that didn't yet have a synagogue for members of

Jewish diaspora, although as women and Gentiles, those worshipers probably would not have had access to the local synagogue, even if there were one.

What the Bible does seem to illustrate is that Lydia had a curious and independent nature in that she was open and willing to learn about new things. Perhaps, in spite of all that she possessed, she was seeking something deeper, a sense of purpose in her life. When she met Paul, her spirit opened to this teaching and preaching about the Good News of Jesus. Within a short time, she was converted and baptized and was moved to have everyone in her household baptized as well. She bears witness to the mandate of Joshua 24:15: "as for me and my household, we will serve the Lord." Lydia earned the title of Paul's first European convert.

A Woman with Chutzpah

Scripture provides a telling description of all of the ways that Lydia's home became the headquarters of the church that Paul established at Philippi. She financially and physically provided a home away from home for Paul and Silas (food, shelter, safety, sanctuary), as well as a home base for the new church to meet and worship.

However, don't miss two major points here. First, for Lydia, a God-fearing Gentile woman, to offer her home and resources to two Jewish men (and their acceptance of that support) was truly radical and a countercultural stretch for all involved. Acts 16:15 gives us a glimpse of Lydia's urging Paul to accept her hospitality when she implores, "If you have judged me to be faithful to the Lord, come and stay at my home." Tacit in that invitation is a challenge to Paul and an offer too good to refuse—to disregard the conventions of the day, accept the offer, and set up a Christian headquarters in Philippi.

Second, Lydia would be taking a real risk in offering her home as Paul and Silas's base of operations. She would be aligning herself and her household with newcomers to the city, a stance which could have professional implications for her. It was a risk that got real all too soon, when Paul and Silas were arrested, flogged, and thrown into prison days later (Act 16:16-34). However, that same Scripture records no negative consequences for Lydia's association with them even as they returned to her home immediately upon their release from prison. This gives us insight into her status, stature, presence, and position in the community. The church at Philippi undoubtedly benefitted from the stability and security her standing in the city ensured. And even if some officials were inclined to look askance at her choice of friends, she probably dealt with them effectively (Acts 16:15).

Spiritual Gifts in Action

When the Apostle Paul spoke of the spiritual gift of hospitality (referred to as "giving" in Romans 12:8), he may have had Lydia in mind. In Romans 12:4-8 and 1 Corinthians 12 and 14, Paul introduces the concept of members of the body of Christ, the church, being empowered with different spiritual gifts that are given to build up, develop, and enhance the quality of life of God's people and the ministry of God's church. These gifts include but are not limited to teaching, preaching, administration, discernment, the ministry of helps (sometimes called encouragement), giving, prophecy, and speaking in tongues. Paul educates us to the fact that everyone has been given a gift—everyone

(Romans 12:7)! Each gift is independent in that it has its own duties and responsibilities to the church. One gift is not considered more valuable than the other. They all have equal importance.

Let's face it. It's doubtful that Lydia woke up one morning and decided on a laundry list of ways and things that she could do to help Paul as he went about establishing the church at Philippi. Odds are good that Lydia's willingness to help, support, and give comfort and aid to Paul were already a major part of her personality. With Paul and the church, she applied and utilized her gift of hospitality in that specific way. Think for a minute about what that great gift meant to Paul, the infant church, and the spread of God's Word!

So it is with you. Your spiritual gifts must be identified and then used in God's house, among God's people, and ultimately in the world beyond those church doors. Again, it not only strengthens the church and the gospel, it also strengthens and empowers us as individuals and as Christians.

Lydia's use of her spiritual gift blessed more people than she could ever imagine. She mentors to us that each and every gift is blessed and valuable in its own way. Your spiritual gift is just as valuable. Pray for clarity to identify it, embrace it, pray for courage to use it, and get to work!

Questions

1. In what ways did Paul, Silas, and the new church at Philippi benefit from Lydia's spiritual gift of hospitality and generosity?
2. In what ways did Lydia benefit from having such a spiritual gift?

3. Read Romans 12:4-8 and 1 Corinthians 12:12-31. Then make a list of the spiritual gifts described in those passages. Which gift describes you? Why?
4. Think about all of the different kinds of ministries in which your church or church family is involved. What is lacking? Why is it lacking?
5. Focusing on you and your spiritual gift, what are some new ways that you can use your gifts?

A Prayer for You

Creator God, we are wondrously blessed to know that when you created us, you thought so carefully about us that just creating us wasn't enough. You thought through the process of giving us abilities, talents, skills, and spiritual gifts, not only to empower us with a rich and meaningful life but also that, through those gifts, we will represent you in the world. So it is with your daughter. Help her to listen, trust, and be obedient to your calling her to the gift and gifts that you have placed within her. Stop her, Lord God, when she would prove to be shy, insecure, or afraid to display that which you have implanted within her. Stir us all up to the point that we know little peace within unless and until we recognize our gifts and step out in faith to accomplish all that you desire for us to accomplish.

Be with your daughter at each and every step she takes in presenting her gift to a world that may question, discourage, or denigrate that which she does. In those days and times, remind her of who you are and what you are in her life: her creator, provider, comforter and her God. In Jesus' name we pray. Amen.

A Prayer from You

21

THE IDEAL WOMAN

A Mentor in Excellence

Proverbs 31:10-31

She is the stuff of Mother's Day cards and a host of Women's Day celebrations and observances in African American churches. The woman of Proverbs 31 is applauded and lauded as the ideal example of excellence for all women. The King James Version calls her "virtuous" (v. 10); other translations describe her as "capable" (NRSV), "competent" (CEB), "excellent" (ESV, NASB), and having "noble character" (NIV). As we read the Scriptures, we discover that she's quite a woman and worthy of being called our mentor.

Story Synopsis

This familiar passage of Scripture begins with the search for a woman whose attributes and qualities comprise a package so total and complete that she is compared with rare and precious jewels! The woman described is a composite character, probably not an actual historic person but a cultural ideal.

The description is compiled by a mother who wants her son to find the perfect spouse to partner him in life. And because the culture in which this ideal is presented is an ancient Israelite one, the assumption is that the ideal woman is married with children.

According to this catalogue of characteristics, the ideal woman is a wife and mother whose husband and children lack for nothing—and of course they are absolutely crazy about her (Proverbs 31:11-12; 28). She's intelligent and wise, a shrewd business woman, hardworking and industrious (vv. 16-18). She minds her own business interests and is admired and respected by everyone who knows her (v. 25). Folks seek her out for her opinions and advice (vv. 26-27). She is honest, loyal, devoted, and compassionate, caring for the poor in the community as well as her own family (vv. 20-21).

This ideal woman is the type of woman who is so together, so capable and trustworthy, that her husband is known and identified in the city by her reputation (Proverbs 31:23). Yes, we can imagine that she is probably physically attractive; however, according to her future mother-in-law, it is her noble character that makes her beautiful and a spouse to cherish (v. 30).

Lessons for Life

Comparing Lists

What woman doesn't have a list of attributes that she is seeking in a future spouse? In fact, too many women are criticized and admonished (check out a few movies and books) for the proverbial laundry lists of stuff that the ideal man needs to have in order for many of these young women to be approached. Qualities such as being tall, athletic, good-looking, employed in a good job, possessing a nice car or a sizeable bank account, having good credit, and having no baby mommas and no experience with the justice system are often at the top of such a list.

Well, darlin', look at this list again. Notice anything or a few things missing? Where are the character traits? Characteristics such as honesty, compassion, trust, humility, a good sense of humor, morals, strong work ethic, a desire to know God. Look closely, because this list of character traits looks and sounds a lot like the list of attributes cited in Proverbs 31 about the ideal woman. Ephesians 5:28 suggests that men and women, husbands and wives should be mirror images of each other, able to complement each other's strengths and compensate (in healthy ways) for the other's weaknesses. So, if we want that ideal man, we ought to be thinking about how to become the ideal woman.

Or perhaps we should stick with the word that appears in the original Hebrew. In total, this portrait of a woman creates an ideal—but the doting mother who put together that list wanted a woman of excellence for her son. And excellence comes in a variety of colors, flavors, and composites. No wonder God admonishes us to seek the Holy Spirit's counsel and direction when choosing a mate. When God makes the match, the resulting couple is a dynamic duo, willing to give the best of themselves to each other for the good of the marriage.

Working Women Take Note!
In Proverbs 31:15-18, we find that our woman of excellence has a lot in common with us today in that she works outside the home. In fact, she is a small business owner, and apparently, quite a good one. Her day starts very early and extends beyond the daylight hours. That's her daily routine and life.

She doesn't beat up on herself about it; she doesn't allow herself to feel guilty or tortured. She just works it. Members of her family are the beneficiaries of her work ethic, but her labor provides a great deal of self-satisfaction as well.

We also know that this sistah had to know something about organization, preparation, and delegation in order to do what she does on a daily basis. Today, we see where organization has become a lifestyle complete with planners, designer calendars, apps. I mean, who knew (other than Franklin Covey?) there was so much money to be made in creating products designed to help a person keep up with daily tasks? (Don't you wish you had thought of that?) And despite the purchase of those items to help us get and stay organized, how many of us don't use them and just do what we've got to do? How many of us (or is it just me?) just grab the back of an envelope to jot down a grocery list or "to do" list? Doesn't Nike say, "Just do it"?

We see something else as well in this passage. This is not a woman who has a lot of idle time. She's not going house to house shooting the breeze and gossiping with her girlfriends (1 Timothy 5:13-14); such women aren't in this sistah's list of personal contacts. She hasn't the time or inclination to be a part of that group. In Proverbs 31:22, we note that in addition to all that she does for others, she sews for herself. Perhaps that is where she finds her "me" time, that precious time of the day where her hands may be busy but her heart and mind thinks (and prays!) about the things in her life that bring her joy and peace. For so many of us, our "me" time translates into doing craft projects—sewing (like her!), knitting, quilting, photography, gardening (Pinterest anyone?), cooking, etc.; those are opportunities to bring our gifts of beauty and creativity into the forefront of our lives, often just for ourselves. And, as it does for the sistah of Proverbs 31, the "me" time restores and nourishes us. So do you have a "me" time? And if not, why not?

A Worthy Mentor

Proverbs 31:31 concludes by letting us know that everything this woman does—her work ethic, her business, her family, the ways that she carries herself, her character—is an example to her community as well as to other women. Verse 15 lets us know that she has a staff (servant girls) for whom she serves as mentor, leading, guiding, directing, and teaching them in the ways that she does her thing. We can only imagine the impact that she has on these young women and what attributes and habits they will incorporate in their own lives and families as a result of having her as mentor. If imitation is the highest form of flattery, our woman of Proverbs 31 is quite an example of excellence to be imitated.

Questions

1. Make a list of all of the characteristics that describe the ideal (or excellent) woman. Highlight the characteristics that you share with her.
2. What does the phrase "a woman who fears the Lord" mean?
3. There are quite a few character attributes in the Bible associated with women. Name at least three of them. Why do you think they are associated with women?
4. According to this description in Proverbs 31, do you know any women like this woman? Send them a thank-you card for serving as mentors for you.

A Prayer for You

Creator God, we look at all of the things you have created in our world that are good and solid and noble, and we say thank you. Thank you for associating such things of beauty and excellence with being a woman. Lord, we ask that you remind your daughter of these attributes when she is surrounded by those who think the opposite. Remind her as she attends school, develops as a student, begins a career of work, and begins her life as a mature adult that you were thinking of her when you created these virtues. Remind her that there is more beauty and honor in the way that she carries herself as your daughter and a woman of God than any designer clothes or accessories. Teach her to stay calm, focused, and assured that if she does her part—lives a life that honors you—that you will indeed reward her in the good things that you have set aside just for her.

Show her that even in her youth and young adulthood, she too stands as an example and mentor for others who are silently, intently watching her and how she goes about living her life, solving problems and moving forward toward you. Breathe on her in the hard times where doubt and fear may overwhelm her. Keep her covered with your grace and your mercy. In Jesus' name we pray. Amen.

A Prayer from You

EPILOGUE

Well, there you have it, my darlin', my Top 20+ mentors among women from the Bible. And yes, I know (I know) that the list could have been twice its length. However, these were women who spoke to me and my spirit. After reading their stories, learning of their strengths, weaknesses, vulnerabilities, joys and sorrow, highs and lows, I was struck by how much they could teach us and have taught me. It became my heart's desire to share them with you. And so I have in these pages. Ain't God good? As for the names that were omitted (yes, sorry, I left her out and her too!), perhaps next time they will be included. May God lead and guide in that direction (volume 2?).

And among the women included and omitted, who makes your Top 20 or Top 10 list of biblical mentors? Why those women? Perhaps that question will serve as a catalyst for discussions between and among you, your friends, sistahs, colleagues, and acquaintances. How many long (long) phone calls, lunches, dinners, and late-night talk sessions would just your list generate? I'm excited at the prospect.

Quite often when I teach a class or facilitate a workshop, I am asked, Why do you write what you write? Initially I found that to be a difficult question to answer because I thought some great psychological or ethical response was required and I knew I wasn't that deep or that smart. Over time and life's many and varied experiences, coupled with massive doses of prayer, I've learned that I write because God has given me the spiritual gifts of encouragement, discernment, and teaching. Additionally, it took Sister Hattie Long, a godly woman, elder, and mentor, to help me understand, realize, and embrace those gifts. Writing is how those gifts have been manifested within me. I must write because I find that what comes up must come out. Will everything that comes up and out become a book? Probably not (in publishing, it's called editing!). However, I encourage you to truly, honestly, and prayerfully investigate your spiritual gifts. The knowledge and utility of those gifts will absolutely change and enrich your life.

Second, when I think about my first book, *The Real Deal: A Spiritual Guide for Black Teen Girls,* and this one, I know that the Spirit chose me to be God's recording secretary because that's what I've done: written what God told me to write. Now, why the Lord chose me out of so many others (wiser, smarter, more intelligent, wittier, etc.) is one of the top 5 questions I intend to ask when I see my Savior on that great day!

Finally, the Word of God is an awesome read! The more we are led to read it, the more we want to read it. You name it, it's in there. No wonder it's called the Book of Life, for it gives us not only truth but also life—a more abundant life. Continue to stay glued to its pages, caught up in its many wonderful stories and truths, and stay tuned as it acts as mentor to teach lessons for all our lives.

Stay blessed and under God's wings,
BMC